the orthodox heretic

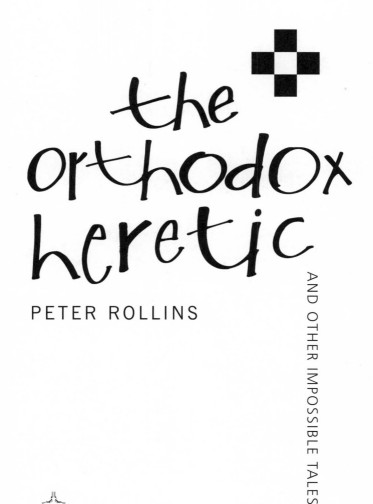

the orthodox heretic

PETER ROLLINS

AND OTHER IMPOSSIBLE TALES

PARACLETE PRESS
BREWSTER MASSACHUSETTS

The Orthodox Heretic and Other Impossible Tales

2010 Second Printing
2009 First Printing

Copyright © 2009 by Peter Rollins

ISBN 978-1-55725-634-8

Library of Congress Cataloging-in-Publication Data
Rollins, Peter.
  The orthodox heretic and other impossible tales / Peter Rollins.
      p. cm.
  Includes bibliographical references.
  ISBN 978-1-55725-634-8
  1. Christian life. 2. Emergent church movement. I. Title.
  BV4515.3.R66 2009
  230--dc22   2008048846

10 9 8 7 6 5 4 3 2

Published by Paraclete Press
Brewster, Massachusetts
www.paracletepress.com

Printed in the United States of America

■ DEDICATION

Most of my closest companions have never read a word I have written. Worse than this, the few who have, see fit to respond with a barrage of abuse (taking great pleasure in finding typos, ill-formed thoughts, and even the faintest hint of hypocrisy). Are these responses not a perfect manifestation of true love? This book is dedicated to them.

CONTENTS

INTRODUCTION

DIS-COURSES
THE SACRED ART OF (MIS)COMMUNICATION

HOW TO SPEAK OF SOMETHING THAT CANNOT BE SAID? Is this dilemma not simultaneously both the obstacle and the opening for those who write of, and wrestle with, the sacred? Is this confrontation with the abyss of the unspeakable not what makes such a writer's job both possible and impossible at the same time, enticing the readers to step beyond, into the beyond where one cannot step?

It is precisely the futility of this pursuit that acts as the manna that sustains such desert pilgrims in their unending quest to inscribe, enact, and incarnate truth. And it is as we lean toward such travelers, listening to the dry crackle of their encrypted, elusive whisperings, that we may catch a glimpse of that truth. This truth can be spoken only by those who live it, and heard only by those who heed it. These timeless incantations have gone by many names over the millennia, but one such name is "parable." In the parable, truth is not expressed via some detached logical discourse that would be employed to educate us, but rather it emanates from the creation of a lyrical *dis*-course that inspires and transforms us—a dis-course being that form of (mis)communication that sends us spinning off course and onto a new course.

The artist knows only too well that infinite abyss out of which the parable arises, as does the revolutionary and the poet in their struggles to speak of that which is born within and yet which remains beyond words. They know this abyss, for it is reflected in their struggle to make straight the paths for the advent of the impossible.

Our religious world is awash with a vast sea of writing and talks designed to make the truth of faith clear, concise, and palatable. For example, one might encounter a talk comprised of three points, all beginning with the letter "p," and all so clear that by the time you leave the room, you will know exactly what to think.

Parables subvert this desire to make faith simple and understandable. They do not offer the reader clarity, for they refuse to be captured in the net of a single interpretation and instead demand our eternal return to their words, our wrestling with them, and our puzzling over them.

This does not mean that the words contain no message, or that they mock us as some insoluble puzzle (and thus not really as a puzzle at all). Parables do not substitute sense for nonsense, or order for disorder. Rather, they point beyond these distinctions, inviting us to engage in a mode of reflection that has less to do with fixing meaning than rendering meaning fluid and affective.

A parable does not primarily provide information about our world. Rather, if we allow it to do its work within us, it will change our world—breaking it open to ever-new possibilities by refusing to be held by the categories that currently exist within that world. In this way the parable transforms the way we hold reality, and thus changes reality itself.

The problem with so much religious communication is that it aims at changing our minds. The result is that we can hear the message of the preacher without necessarily heeding the message; we can listen to the "truth" and agree with it, yet not change in response to it. To use an example, many of us have had a conversation with someone about how accumulating wealth does not bring happiness, about how working all the hours God sends is not healthy, and that owning bigger and better cars is damaging, not only to the soul, but to the world. But then, after the conversation, those involved turn round and act *as if they believed these things*.

In contrast, parables represent a mode of communicating that cannot be heard without being heeded, in which the only evidence of having "heard" its message is in the fleshly incarnation of that message. The parable is heard only when it changes one's social standing to the current reality, not one's mere reflection of it. The parable does not create more self-aware purveyors of irony—whereby one mocks the very behavior that one engages in, thus enjoying the activity in the very moment of disavowing it. (A concrete example of irony would be attending an 80s party dressed up in the clothes of the era, laughing at how ridiculous the clothes and music are, while simultaneously wearing the clothes and dancing to the music.) Rather, the parable facilitates genuine change at the level of action itself. The message is thus hidden in the very words that express it, only to be found by the one who is wholly changed by it. In the words of one great Storyteller, the parable can be heard only by those with ears to hear.

Because of this, I hesitate to call what I have written within these pages *parables* at all and have thus, in the title, opted for the safer word *tales*. It is not for me to christen these short stories with the name *parables*, for who am I to say that they will do the job that I have called them into being to perform? For some they may be parables, while for others they may be nothing but a string of inconsequential stories. For just as one person's idol is another's icon, so one person's fable is another's parable.

The format of this book is simple. I have provided a series of short stories gathered together under three headings: "Beyond Belief," "G-O-D-I-S-N-O-W-H-E-R-E," and "Transfigurations." Each of the stories is followed by a small commentary that is designed to act as a guide for the reader. These small commentaries do not, however, expose the "truth" of the story, nor are they the final word or necessarily of more standing than someone else's careful and thoughtful interpretation. The tales contained here are pregnant with possibilities and, like a child, have the potential to grow beyond what I hoped for, imagined possible, or even desired. As such, it is helpful to approach these commentaries in the same manner as one might approach the descriptions that are often found beside a painting in an art museum. These descriptions are not designed to explain the art, as if the art were somehow incomplete or incompetent, but rather act as a means of providing a place of entry for the uninitiated.

The stories that follow will benefit from a slow and careful reading, a difficult thing for us to do today. We are so accustomed to reading quickly in a desire to consume the information, integrate it, and move on. Books that cannot be read quickly, that withhold themselves from us, are often cast aside in frustration rather than embraced as deep caverns that house treasures for those who persevere. Good books can rarely be scanned quickly and never exhaust themselves in a single reading. Difficult as this may be for us, one paragraph carefully mined from the pages of a good book will yield more wealth than we could possibly collect from a wall of mediocre ones. So it will help greatly, while reading this collection of stories, to take a little time in silence before approaching each of them and some time of reflection afterward, rather than mechanically moving through them in one or two sittings.

To conclude this short introduction, I would like to point out that each of the tales in this book represents my own attempt to explore and testify to the impossible Event housed in faith. In that sense they are deeply personal and relative to my own life. And yet, the more carefully one speaks of one's own journey, the more universal the message can become. So, I find myself compelled to end with a prayer of sorts, one in which I express my hope that these tiny tales will become more than mere words on a page to you the reader, perhaps even becoming worthy of the title *parable*. But, at the end of the day, that is for you to decide.

PART ONE

BEYOND BELIEF ■

1

NO CONVICTION

IN A WORLD WHERE FOLLOWING CHRIST IS DECREED TO BE A SUBVERSIVE AND ILLEGAL ACTIVITY you have been accused of being a believer, arrested, and dragged before a court.

You have been under clandestine surveillance for some time now, and so the prosecution has been able to build up quite a case against you. They begin the trial by offering the judge dozens of photographs that show you attending church meetings, speaking at religious events, and participating in various prayer and worship services. After this, they present a selection of items that have been confiscated from your home: religious books that you own, worship CDs, and other Christian artifacts. Then they step up the pace by displaying many of the poems, pieces of prose, and journal entries that you had lovingly written concerning your faith. Finally, in closing, the prosecution offers your Bible to the judge.

This is a well-worn book with scribbles, notes, drawings, and underlinings throughout, evidence, if it were needed, that you had read and reread this sacred text many times.

Throughout the case you have been sitting silently in fear and trembling. You know deep in your heart that with the large body of evidence that has been amassed by the prosecution you face the possibility of a long imprisonment or even execution. At various times throughout the proceedings you have lost all confidence and have been on the verge of standing up and denying Christ. But while this thought has plagued your mind throughout the trial, you resist the temptation and remain focused.

Once the prosecution has finished presenting their case the judge proceeds to ask if you have anything to add, but you remain silent and resolute, terrified that if you open your mouth, even for a moment, you might deny the charges made against you. Like Christ, you remain silent before your accusers. In response you are led outside to wait as the judge ponders your case.

The hours pass slowly as you sit under guard in the foyer waiting to be summoned back.

Eventually a young man in uniform appears and leads you into the courtroom so that you may hear the verdict and receive word of your punishment. Once you have been seated in the dock the judge, a harsh and unyielding man, enters the room, stands before you, looks deep into your eyes and begins to speak.

"Of the charges that have been brought forward I find the accused *not guilty*."

"Not guilty?" your heart freezes. Then, in a split second, the fear and terror that had moments before threatened to strip your resolve are swallowed up by confusion and rage.

Despite the surroundings, you stand defiantly before the judge and demand that he give an account concerning why you are innocent of the charges in light of the evidence.

"What evidence?" he replies in shock.

"What about the poems and prose that I wrote?" you reply.

"They simply show that you think of yourself as a poet, nothing more."

"But what about the services I spoke at, the times I wept in church and the long, sleepless nights of prayer?"

"Evidence that you are a good speaker and actor, nothing more," replied the judge. "It is obvious that you deluded those around you, and perhaps at times you even deluded yourself, but this foolishness is not enough to convict you in a court of law."

"But this is madness!" you shout. "It would seem that no evidence would convince you!"

"Not so," replies the judge as if informing you of a great, long-forgotten secret.

"The court is indifferent toward your Bible reading and church attendance; it has no concern for worship with words and a pen. Continue to develop your theology, and use it to paint pictures of love. We have no interest in such armchair artists who spend their time creating images of a better world. We exist only for those who would lay down that brush, and their life, in a Christlike endeavor to create a better world. So, until you live as Christ and his followers did, until you challenge this system and become a thorn in our side, until you die to yourself and offer your body to the flames, until then, my friend, you are no enemy of ours."

COMMENTARY

This reflection was written after I happened to see a car speed past with a bumper sticker that read, "If Christianity were illegal would there be enough evidence to convict you?" At the time, I didn't pay this little saying much thought, but over the course of the day it began to take root in my consciousness and play on my mind. So that evening I took some time to imagine such a world and what would happen to me if I lived in it. I was not interested in imagining a world where Christianity as a mere tradition or belief system was illegal but rather in a place where a life that reflected the acts and teachings of Jesus was prohibited.

Yet, in the process of reflecting I began to wonder whether we actually already lived in such a world. Rather than reading, "If Christianity were illegal would there be enough evidence to convict you?"—I wondered whether the bumper sticker I had seen that day should actually have read, *Christianity is illegal: is there enough evidence to convict you?* For if I were really to take the teachings of Jesus seriously, would I not, sooner or later, find myself being dragged before the authorities? If I were really to live a life that reflected the subversive and radical message of love that gives a voice to the voiceless and a place to those who are displaced, if I were really to stand up against the systemic oppression perpetrated by those in power, then would I not find myself on the wrong side of the lawmakers?

The above story simply exposes the reality of Christ's subversive teaching by imagining that those who exist in the place of power today are both aware of the fact that they oppose the way of Christ and willing to openly admit it. The story thus has two primary points. First, I used it to express the idea that authentic faith is expressed, not in the mere acceptance of a belief system, but in sacrificial, loving action. Here I reject the inner/outer distinction in which one can fool oneself into thinking that private beliefs are somehow more important or reflective of one's essence than public actions. Second, I wished to draw the reader into the reflection that perhaps this larger-than-life scenario, in its imaginary description of an alternative universe, is actually merely a reflection of the universe that we already inhabit. By creating a fictional world, we thus come face-to-face with our own world.

JESUS AND THE FIVE THOUSAND
(A FIRST-WORLD TRANSLATION)

JESUS WITHDREW PRIVATELY BY BOAT TO A SOLITARY PLACE, but the crowds continued to follow him. Evening was now approaching and the people, many of whom had traveled a great distance, were growing hungry.

Seeing this, Jesus sent his disciples out to gather food, but all they could find were five loaves of bread and two fishes. Then Jesus asked that they go out again and gather up the provisions that the crowds had brought to sustain them in their travels. Once this was accomplished, a vast mountain of fish and bread stood before Jesus. Upon seeing this he directed the people to sit down on the grass.

Standing before the food and looking up to heaven, he gave thanks to God and broke the bread. Then he passed the food among his twelve disciples. Jesus and his friends ate like kings in full view of the starving people. But what was truly amazing, what was miraculous about this meal, was that when they had finished the massive banquet there were not even enough crumbs left to fill a starving person's hand.

COMMENTARY

The initial shock of this story relates to the way that it inscribes selfish and inhumane actions onto Christ himself by twisting the story we all know of Jesus feeding the multitude. While it would seem perfectly acceptable to attack governments, corporations, and individuals for failing to distribute goods appropriately and turning away from the poorest among us who suffer as a direct result of our greed, it would seem inappropriate to read such inhumanity into the actions of Christ himself. If anything, Christ was one who demonstrated a life of joyful simplicity, radical healing, and unimaginable love. Christ challenges us to look outward, and thus he should not be the one whom we condemn.

Yet in the Bible we read that those who follow Christ are nothing less than the manifestation of his body in the world today (Colossians 1:24, 1 Corinthians 12:27, and Ephesians 5:30). The presence of Christ in the world is said to be directly encountered in the presence of those who gather together in his name. In very concrete terms, people learn of Christ through those who claim to live out the way of Christ. However, if Christ is proclaimed in the life of his followers, if the body of believers is thought to manifest the body of Christ in the world, then we must stop, draw breath, and ask ourselves whether the above tale reflects how Christ is presented to the world today, at least in the minds of those who witness the lifestyle of Christians in the West.

TRANSLATING THE WORD
(ADAPTED FROM A BUDDHIST PARABLE)

IT HAS BEEN SAID THAT MANY YEARS AGO THERE LIVED A YOUNG AND GIFTED WOMAN CALLED SOPHIA who received a vision in which God spoke to her as a dear friend. In this conversation God asked that Sophia dedicate her life to the task of translating and distributing the Word of God throughout her country. Now, at this time the printing press had only recently been invented, and the only Bibles to be found were written in Latin and kept under lock and key within churches. Sophia was from a poor farming village on the outskirts of the city, so the task seemed impossible. She would have to raise a vast sum of money to purchase the necessary printing equipment, rent a building to house it, and hire scholars with the ability to translate the Latin verses into the country's common tongue.

However, the impossibility of the task did not sway her in the least. After having received her vision, Sophia sold the few items she possessed and left the village to live on the streets of the city, begging for the money that was required and dedicating herself to any work that was available in order to help with the funds.

Raising the money proved to be a long and difficult task, for while there were a few who gave generously, most only gave little, if anything at all. In addition to this, living on the streets involved great personal suffering. But gradually, over the next fifteen years, the money began to accumulate.

Shortly before the plans for the printing press could be set in motion, a dreadful flood devastated a nearby town, destroying many people's homes and livelihood. When the news reached Sophia she gathered up what she had raised and spent it on food for the hungry, material to help rebuild lost homes, and basic provisions for the dispossessed.

Eventually the town began to recover from the natural disaster that had befallen it and so Sophia left and returned to the city in order to start over again, all the while remembering the vision that God had planted deep in her heart.

Many more years passed slowly, extracting their heavy toll on the beautiful Sophia. But there were now many who had been touched by her love and dedication, so although people were poor, the money began to accumulate once again. However, after nine more years, disaster struck again. This time a plague descended upon the city, stealing the lives of thousands and leaving many children without family or support.

By now Sophia was tired and very ill, yet without hesitation she used the money that had been collected to buy medicines for the sick, homes for the orphaned, and land where the dead could be buried safely.

Never once did she forget the vision that God had imparted to her, but the severity of the plague required that she set this sacred call to one side in order to help with the emergency. Only when the shadow of the plague had lifted did she once again take to the streets, driven by her desire to translate the Word of God and distribute it among the people.

Finally, shortly before her death, Sophia was able to gather together the money required for the printing press, the building, and the translators.

Although she was, by this time, close to death, Sophia lived long enough to see the first Bibles printed and distributed.

It is said to this day that Sophia had actually accomplished her task of translating and distributing the Word of God three times during her life rather than simply once—the first two being more beautiful and radiant than the last.

COMMENTARY

Here we are invited to reflect upon the true meaning of the phrase *Word of God*. While this term is often used in order to describe a set of Scriptures, the above tale asks the reader whether words in a book, no matter how beautifully constructed, could ever be worthy of such a title. Of course, for many the Bible is worthy of this hallowed title. The words, or at least the message contained by the words, has a status far beyond that of even the greatest literary achievements. But we must ask whether holding the words of the Bible in such high regard is really the best way to show our love and respect to this ancient text.

For is it not the Bible itself that informs us how God's Word never returns empty (Isaiah 55:11)? In other words, God's holy Word can never fall on deaf ears, but will always evoke transformation in those who truly hear it.

If this is the case, then God's Word cannot be heard without being heeded; it cannot be received without being incarnated. Indeed, it is only in being incarnated that one can say that it has been received. For instance, the words *love your neighbor* should not be thought of as sacred or divine. These words are no more than words. They take on a revelatory role only when they are lived, that is, when someone actually gets their hands dirty and loves their neighbor—in other words, when this phrase is incarnated in action. The idea of loving one's neighbor is the Word of God, not when it is merely affirmed, but when it is lived.

Therefore, it is impossible to affirm God's Word apart from becoming that Word, apart from being the place where that Word becomes a living, breathing act. This divine Word cannot then be rendered into an object that is somehow separate from the subject who hears it or reads it, for the Word of God is an incarnated Word that is lived. Its call is heard only by those who inhale the aroma of the words and who exhale life, liberation, and love.

By attempting to describe this Word we will always end up describing something less than it, for, like love, the Word is discovered not in speech but in act. The Word is formed only when it is performed; it exists in the world only when it is lived out by a subject who dwells fully in the world. Is this not the logic of incarnation?

4

TURNING THE OTHER CHEEK

WE STOOD AT A DISTANCE, WATCHING. We looked on silently as Jesus took his place on the top of a mound, waiting patiently for those who had gathered to settle themselves. We looked with a certain displeasure and discomfort at the disorderly mob that surrounded him. There must have been hundreds of people pushing in to hear his words, most of them poor and hungry. The place was brimming over with the sick and the dispossessed, the widow and the orphan, the ones without a voice and without hope. We watched as Jesus looked at them with compassion and prayed peace into their lives. As he stood before them, we heard him pronounce blessing upon those who are poor in spirit, for those who are mourning, for those who are meek, for those who are merciful despite their hardships, those who are pure in spirit, and upon those who seek peace rather than war.

But Jesus also challenged them saying, "Love your enemies, do good to those who hate you, bless those who curse you, pray for those who mistreat you." He said to them, "If someone strikes you on one cheek, turn to him the other also. If someone takes your cloak, do not stop him from taking your tunic. If someone forces you to carry their pack one mile, carry it two. Give to everyone who asks you, and if anyone takes what belongs to you, do not demand it back." Then he finished by saying, "Do to others as you would have them do to you. Do not judge, and you will not be judged. Do not condemn, and you will not be condemned. Forgive, and you will be forgiven."

When he had finished, he turned toward the west, where we were sitting, we who have the power, who have the authority, and who have a voice. For a time he just stared at us, then he approached and addressed us directly: "Do not be mistaken, these words are not for you."

Then Jesus raised his voice and said, "I am sending you an infinitely more difficult message."

A time is coming when those you now treat as enemies and slaves will show you nothing but love in return, when those who you curse with indifference will offer you blessing. When you slap these people on the right check, be prepared, for they will turn their left check toward you. When you steal their cloak, they will offer you their tunic. And when you demand that they carry your possessions for one mile, they will freely carry those possessions for two. They will give freely what you demand from them, and they will not seek to gain back what you have stolen from them. They will treat you as they would long to be treated. You will judge them but they will not judge you. You will condemn them but they will not condemn you.

Before leaving us he finished by saying, "These people are my message to you. Heed this message and you will live. Ignore it, and you will perish."

COMMENTARY

Whenever we open up our Bible and read that Jesus commands us to love those who hate us, bless those who curse us, and repay evil with kindness, it is easy to apply this to our daily interaction with others. However, these teachings were not given to people like us (by *us* I mean people who can afford to buy this book and are educated enough to be able to read it). These were not spoken primarily for the powerful to apply as middle-class moral platitudes. They were spoken to the powerless, whose country was under occupation and whose very lives were under constant threat. It is likely that, like me, you do not face the kind of persecution that Jesus' original listeners faced. Indeed the unpalatable truth may well be that we are the ones who oppress the type of people that Jesus spoke with—not directly with hatred in our hearts, but indirectly through the clothes we buy, the coffee we drink, the investments we make, and the cars that we drive. By reading these words in an affluent, Western setting we can so easily domesticate the words of Jesus to the extent that they become little more than advice on how to treat a shop assistant or a passerby.

In the above story I attempt to undermine the reduction of Christ's words to the level of inane politeness by drawing out how the words are directed toward the oppressed rather than toward the oppressors. In this way I am attempting to remind myself that these words are spoken to those people whom I hurt and destroy through the choices I make on a daily basis, and that I am merely overhearing them. In the above story, I ask myself to imagine what Jesus would say to me if I had been there at the time. Would he address me with the words "If someone takes your cloak, give them your tunic as well"? Or would he be more likely to address me with the admonition "Stop stealing from the poor"?

5

SALVATION FOR A DEMON

IN THE CENTER OF A ONCE-GREAT CITY THERE STOOD A MAGNIFICENT CATHEDRAL that was cared for by a kindly old priest who spent his days praying in the vestry and caring for the poor. As a result of the priest's tireless work, the cathedral was known throughout the land as a true sanctuary. The priest welcomed all who came to his door and gave completely without prejudice or restraint. Each stranger was, to the priest, a neighbor in need and thus the incoming of Christ. His hospitality was famous and his heart was known to be pure. No one could steal from this old man, for he considered no possession his own, and while thieves sometimes left that place with items pillaged from the sanctuary, the priest never grew concerned: he had given everything to God and knew that these people needed such items more than the church did.

Early one evening in the middle of winter, while the priest was praying before the cross, there was a loud and ominous knock on the cathedral door. The priest quickly got to his feet and went to the entrance, as he knew it was a terrible night and reasoned that his visitor might be in need of shelter.

Upon opening the door he was surprised to find a terrifying demon towering over him with large dead eyes and rotting flesh.

"Old man," the demon hissed, "I have traveled many miles to seek your shelter. Will you welcome me in?"

Without hesitation, the priest bid this hideous demon welcome and beckoned him into the church. The evil demon stooped down and stepped across the threshold, spitting venom onto the tiled floor as he went. In full view of the priest, the demon proceeded to tear down the various icons that adorned the walls and rip the fine linens that hung around the sanctuary, while screaming blasphemy and curses.

During this time the priest knelt silently on the floor and continued in his devotions until it was time for him to retire for the night.

"Old man," cried the demon, "where are you going now?"

"I am returning home to rest, for it has been a long day," replied the kindly priest.

"May I come with you?" spat the demon. "I too am tired and in need of a place to lay my head."

"Why, of course," replied the priest. "Come, and I will prepare a meal."

On returning to his house, the priest prepared some food while the evil demon mocked the priest and broke the various religious artifacts that adorned his humble dwelling. The demon then ate the meal that was provided and afterward turned his attention to the priest,

"Old man, you welcomed me first into your church and then into your house. I have one more request for you: will you now welcome me into your heart?"

"Why, of course," said the priest, "what I have is yours and what I am is yours."

This heartfelt response brought the demon to a standstill, for by giving everything the priest had retained the very thing that the demon sought to take. For the demon was unable to rob him of his kindness and his hospitality, his love and his compassion. And so the great demon left in defeat, never to return.

What happened to that demon after this meeting with the elderly priest is anyone's guess. Some say that although he left that place empty-handed he received more than he could ever have imagined.

And the priest? He simply ascended his stairs, got into bed and drifted off to sleep, all the time wondering what guise his Christ would take next.

COMMENTARY

The first thing to note about this story is that it expresses an impossible hospitality, a hospitality that flings open its doors to anyone, without condition. In contrast to this, our own hospitality is conditional and is generally extended only to those we like or to those who will abide by certain rules of etiquette. Our hospitality is often little more than a self-interested exchange whereby we invite some people to our house for our own pleasure. There are conditions to our hospitality, conditions that include politeness, respect, and a nice bottle of wine.

While there is nothing wrong with such a situation, the radical, impossible hospitality spoken of by Christ is one that goes infinitely further than this. It is a hospitality that opens the doors to those who are not part of our friendship circle, those who are not likely to bring us gifts or respect our sensibilities. This view of hospitality resonates with Jesus' view of love, a love that asks us to do more than simply embrace those who love us (something that even the most heartless criminals do). It asks us to embrace those who are indifferent to us or who even despise us. This is wonderfully expressed in Jesus' description of a wedding feast in which the doors of the party are opened to passers-by—to anyone who would want to come. This radical hospitality manifests itself as an unconditional gift rather than as a conditional exchange. Here the outsiders are welcomed in, the excluded are the ones who are included.

This type of hospitality will strike us as utterly impossible and even offensive for a variety of reasons, perhaps because we selfishly want to protect our new carpets or maybe because we selflessly need to protect our family. However, it is precisely the impossible nature of divine hospitality that we must bear in mind when we encounter others. For it helps to remind us that we can never pat ourselves on the back and claim that we have been truly hospitable, that we have somehow reflected the radical nature of Christ in our actions. This impossible vision of divine hospitality can also inspire us to act in a more generous and gracious manner than we might otherwise be inclined toward—remembering that God has opened the doors to us and that we should endeavor to do the same.

To welcome the demon, in whatever form the demon takes, is all but impossible. But through our trying to show hospitality to the demon at our door, the demon may well be transformed by the grace that is shown. Or, we may come to realize that it was not really a demon at all, but just a broken, damaged person like ourselves.

6

THE PEARL OF GREAT PRICE

A CROWD HAD GATHERED BY THE SHORES OF GALILEE to catch a glimpse of Jesus and to hear him speak. People from all walks of life had turned up, from the powerful to the powerless, the rich to the poor, the healthy to the sick. Jesus looked upon them with compassion and began to speak of God's kingdom. Then from among the assembled people a man dressed in fine clothes shouted out, "Tell us Lord, to what would you compare the kingdom of God?"

Jesus paused for a moment before looking out towards the sea.

"Let me tell a story," he replied. "There was once a rich merchant who spent his days searching for fine pearls. Then one day he found a pearl of such beauty that he immediately went away and sold everything that he possessed so that he would have enough to purchase it. This pearl is like the kingdom."

The crowd looked satisfied with this definition of the kingdom, especially the rich young man who had asked the question, for it addressed itself to the desire that lay deep in his heart.

This kingdom must really be valuable, he thought to himself, *if a wealthy merchant would sell everything that he had in order to possess it.*

While all this was going on, however, there was a young woman who stood at a distance from the crowd listening intently to what Jesus had said, all the time with a smile on her face.

Jesus turned from the crowd and walked toward this unknown spectator. Then he spoke to the woman, saying, "Others listen to what I say, yet fail to hear, for the noise of their heart's desire drowns out my meaning. They forever listen but never understand.

"You, however, have listened and understood."

"All I know," said the young woman, "is that if this kingdom you speak of is like that priceless pearl, then the sacrifice needed in order to grasp it will not make one rich but rather will reduce the one who has sacrificed to absolute poverty. For you are saying that one must give up everything for the pearl, yet the pearl is itself worth nothing unless you find someone to buy it. And if you do find someone then you will no longer have the pearl. So although you may appear to be the richest person alive while you have the pearl, in reality you will have nothing to live on until you give it up."

"Yes," Jesus replied.

"What use then is this pearl?" replied the woman.

"Well," replied Jesus, "the pearl has no value if all you seek is its value. But if you renounce the value of the pearl and give up everything simply because you are captivated by its beauty, then, and only then, will you discover its true value."

■

COMMENTARY   ■

This story is inspired by a reflection by the philosopher Søren Kierkegaard and explores the deeper meaning of Jesus' parable concerning the pearl of great price. Upon first encountering the story one could be struck by the seemingly self-centered motivation of the one who sells everything she has in order to possess the pearl.

It would initially seem that Jesus is directly appealing to people's selfishness and greed. For the merchant gives up the little wealth he already has in order to possess something worth infinitely more. This effectively reduces the kingdom of God to an economy in which one thing is given so as to procure another. But is it really possible to sacrifice something if we know that we are going to receive something of even greater value in return? Does the person who agrees to give a grain of sand in exchange for a diamond really sacrifice anything at all?

Of course, someone may respond by saying that this is exactly what we find proclaimed in the Bible. But is this really the case? Let us take an example from the Gospels, namely the calling of the first disciples. When Jesus first called the disciples they would have had little information about Jesus, except perhaps that he was a controversial rabbi. Yet, they responded to his call by giving up their families and livelihood to follow him. Only after they made this sacrifice and lived with him for some time did Jesus finally comfort them with stories of how their sacrifice had not gone unnoticed and of how they would gain a great reward for what they had laid down. Here we see how the sacrifice came before the promise of reward, and was thus real sacrifice.

However, today, this order is often reversed so that a person will first hear about the reward of following Christ as an incentive to give their life as a living sacrifice. Instead of giving up everything out of sacrificial love and then indirectly discovering the wealth that such an act opens up, we are encouraged to "sacrifice" as a way of directly attaining the wealth of faith. But this attempt at directly grasping the wealth of the kingdom only ensures that we become the poorest of all. In the logic of faith it is only by renouncing the wealth directly, saying, "I do not care about what I get from this sacrifice; all I want is you," that we discover the wealth indirectly.

It is in this way that we should approach the story of the pearl of great price: understanding that if we were to sell everything that we possessed in order to own a priceless pearl, then we would become the poorest of all, having nothing of value except for the pearl itself. We would not be able to purchase food or pay for shelter. We would be destitute. The only thing we would be able to do would be to sell the pearl. But then we would no longer have the pearl.

The paradox of the pearl lies in the idea that, in becoming the poorest of all, we simultaneously become the richest of all. The poverty is not then a first step toward the treasure; rather, the poverty is the very place where we find it. Hence, we can make the rather counterintuitive claim that, in the realm of faith, it is only in renouncing our desire for wealth that we discover it.

7

GREAT MISFORTUNE

THERE WAS ONCE AN OLD MAN NAMED BENONI who had known great misfortune through life, having lost his wife and children to poverty, disease, and war. The many lines on his face betrayed his pain, and his heart was filled with sorrow and regret. Indeed he barely had the strength to carry on.

But there was one who had drawn alongside him in his sorrow. His comforter was the village blacksmith, a strong but caring man who exhibited a gentle, humble, and charitable way of life. People knew very little about this blacksmith, as he was a quiet man who had moved into the town only a few years before. Yet he was well liked by the community and would often be found sitting on the porch of his workshop, enjoying the midday sun and passing the time by engaging strangers in conversation. His face was strong and full of character, betraying both a depth of spirit and a breadth of experience. But it was also a kindly face that was set alight by his compassionate smile.

When Benoni lost his first child, the blacksmith called round to his home, put his hand on Benoni's shoulder and with great affection said, "I am so sorry that you have suffered this grave misfortune. If you will allow me, I would like to stand with you at this time of hardship."

Ever since this first encounter the blacksmith had called round to Benoni's house most evenings, sometimes to sit and chat, sometimes to listen, and sometimes simply to leave food and other provisions. As each new calamity befell Benoni, the blacksmith would be there to speak and cry with.

One day when Benoni was particularly depressed he went to visit a pastor who lived in the heart of the city, so as to talk through what had taken place over the traumatic years and try to make sense of it. The pastor listened to what Benoni had to say and then, after a little thought, replied, "Well my son, in order for great fortune to take place one must first suffer great misfortune.

The suffering you have faced is the price that has had to be extracted for strength of character, and a spirit forged in the fires of hell."

So Benoni returned to his home alone, lit a fire in an attempt to take away the evening's chill, and contemplated the words of the minister. *Perhaps he is right*, thought Benoni, *maybe I should take some comfort from these words. But it is cold, I am alone, and words can offer no shoulder to rest on.*

Just then the blacksmith knocked on the door and Benoni, as always, welcomed him in. As they sat together they drank whiskey and talked long into the night. That evening Benoni shared the words of the pastor with his friend, adding, "Perhaps now that I have been given these words to comfort me, you no longer need to visit as you have done this last year."

The blacksmith simply looked at the floor for a few moments and then replied, "My dear friend, if what the elder has said is true then I am needed all the more, for if you had to suffer such great misfortune in order to find strength of character and wealth of spirit, then this is in itself a great misfortune."

And so they sat late into the night bringing comfort and warmth to each other through the sharing of their lives.

COMMENTARY

It is sometimes claimed that, while questioning and uncertainty have a place in the life of faith, they are not useful for those who are suffering from pain and anxiety. At these times it is often said that people require certainties, and that it is the church's role to provide them. Apart from the fact that this view can seem a little patronizing, for it suggests that people need simple answers when they are in pain because they would not be able to handle anything else, we must ask whether certainty is something that really brings comfort to the distressed.

In order to explore this let us borrow a distinction offered by the Jewish philosopher Emmanuel Levinas between the *saying* and the *said*. When one speaks there is both the *act* of saying and the *content* that is communicated. These are intimately united in our everyday speech and are rarely distinguished. However we can, if we sit back and reflect, note how our speech involves both sounds and the information that these sounds convey. This distinction becomes clearer when we think of meeting someone who speaks a language that we do not understand. For here we become aware that the person is saying something, but we are unsure of what is being said.

In academic life the *said* is often privileged over the *saying*. What is important is that meaning is communicated and, as such, the way it is communicated is important only insomuch as it gets the meaning across. Yet there are forms of communication that give emphasis to the saying over and above the said.

An interesting example of this can be seen at work in the music of Sigur Rós, a band from Iceland that employs what they call "Vonlenska" (or "Hoplandic") in many of their songs. "Vonlenska" sounds like a language, however it lacks consistent grammar, logical structure, meaningful syllables, and often even discrete words. When a song is sung in Vonlenska, the words that you hear do not "mean" anything; nothing is said in their saying.

Yet the saying itself invites a change in the sensitive listener. In contemplating the music, one touches upon a deep reservoir of emotion that emanates from the song. This mode of "communication" is similar to what we see taking place between an infant and its parents. The grammatical nonsense that is communicated by the infant to the parent and by the parent to the infant is a discourse in which nothing is said, but a connection is established or deepened.

When we are facing difficult situations is it not true that the pastoral act is not one that offers some explanation for the suffering (the said) but rather is found in the act of one who offers presence to the other in the form of words and gestures (the saying)? Here it is not an explanation that brings healing and comfort, but rather the fact that someone is interacting with us, the fact that someone loves us and stands with us. What brings comfort is the fact that there is proximity to another and presence with another. It is the fact that flesh touches flesh and the gaze of the one who suffers meets the gaze of the one who cares. This act of gentle presence is balm for the wounded soul.

Here, at the level of the saying, religious language truly flowers. For the language of faith is not primarily interested in communicating information (Jesus did not come as a scientist or a theologian), but in forming healthy, healing, transformative relationships. Giving someone a "reason" for suffering and a promise that things will work out in the end should never be confused with communicating the truth of faith. When faced with situations like the Holocaust, or modern-day genocides, it is offensive to offer reasons for the horror (such as a divine test or punishment). Here the response of the faithful is not to be found in the offering of a theodicy but in drawing alongside those who suffer, and fighting on their behalf. The truth of faith is not articulated in offering reasons for suffering, but rather in drawing alongside those who suffer, standing with them, and standing up for them. This is pastoral care at its most luminous.

8

THE THIRD MILE

ONE DAY A SMALL GROUP OF DISCIPLES WHO HAD EMBRACED THE WAY OF JESUS EARLY IN HIS MINISTRY HEARD HIM PREACHING by the side of a dusty road. As they crowded round they heard Jesus say,

"The law requires that you carry a pack for one mile, but I say carry it freely for two."

The disciples were deeply impressed by these words, for at that time a Roman soldier had the legal right to demand that a citizen carry his pack for a mile as a service to the Empire. This teaching not only allowed the disciples to turn this oppressive law into an opportunity to demonstrate kingdom values, but also presented them with an opportunity to suffer in some small way for their faith.

As it was common for soldiers to evoke this law, the small band of believers soon developed a reputation for their actions. Roman soldiers would often hope that the citizens they asked to carry their packs would be among these disciples, and often a small bond of friendship would develop between a soldier and these followers of the Way.

After a year had passed this custom had become so established in the group that it became a defining characteristic of their shared life. The leaders would frequently refer to the teaching of Jesus and emphasize the need to carry a pack of the Roman soldier for two miles as a sign of one's faith and commitment to God.

It so happened that Jesus heard about this community's work, and, on his way to Jerusalem, took time to visit them. The leaders eagerly gathered all the members of the group to hear what Jesus would say. Once everyone had gathered, Jesus addressed them:

"Dear brothers and sisters, you are faithful and honest, but I have come to you with a second message, for you failed to understand the first. Your law says that you must carry a pack for two miles. My law says, 'carry it for three.'"

COMMENTARY

To treat the Bible as a type of textbook providing us with an ethical blueprint concerning how we ought to live, requires that we approach it in a certain way. It means that we must attempt to excavate specific answers, or some system, from the text that will direct what we should do in particular situations. Once the answers are worked out, then we can choose whether or not to act accordingly and judge whether others are making the correct ethical decisions. Yet the question must be asked as to whether the Bible can be treated in this way without doing the teachings of Jesus a great injustice. In other words, we must ask whether the Scriptures really offer us concrete ethical answers that can be turned into some religious code of conduct, or whether Jesus was actually opening up a radically different approach to living.

What if Jesus was not offering his followers an ethical system to follow, but rather was inviting them to enter into a life of love that transcends ethics, a life of liberty that dwells beyond religious laws? The difference between following an ethical system and being consumed by love can be seen in the way that ethical systems seek to provide a way to work out what needs to be done so that it can be carried out. In contrast, love is never constrained, it never sits back, it always seeks to do more than what is demanded of it. While the ethical individual does what is required, the lover moves beyond the basic requirement. To put this in concrete terms, if the law tells us that one ought to give a certain amount of money to charity, the one who loves those who are poor will give more than the required amount. Instead of waiting to find out what ought to be done, or how much should be given, the lover gives in excess of the law and will act in the absence of the law, thus fulfilling the law by dwelling beyond it.

The above story explores this idea by imagining what Jesus would say to those who had taken his teaching about carrying a pack two miles literally, seeing it as an ethical injunction and a religious law. In their very obedience to the teaching, the group described in the story fundamentally misunderstood and undermined the radical

nature of the message. Their literal rendering
of the teaching, far from taking it too seriously,
ended up failing to take it seriously enough.

It would be wrong to condemn the disciples in
this story, for they were trying to do something
rather than nothing. However, a real danger lurks
in the sincere attempt to carry out the teaching
of Jesus in a literal manner, namely the danger
of absorbing his way of living in excess of the
law back into the law. The radical way of Jesus
provides a much more difficult challenge than
that which is demanded by the law. For while the
law gives us a bottom-line way to live, the way of
love calls us beyond the law.

Love pushes us beyond duty, rather than
stopping there, and acts when we don't know for
sure what the ethical thing to do is. If the ethical
question is, "What must be done?" love adds,
"I will do more." If our ethical compass is not
able to give us a clear direction to travel, love
sets out anyway. The way of love provides a way
when ethical demands have had their say or do
not know what to say. Is this not what Jesus was
calling us to?—to live beyond the law so as to
fulfill it.

In this way this story attempts to draw out the truly radical nature of love as expressed in the life and teachings of Jesus. For he expressed a love that pushed further than any law could express or command dictate. He exuded a revolutionary life that always sought to be faithful to the law by outstripping it.

9

THE INVISIBLE PROPHET

IT IS SAID THAT WHEN GOD SENT ONE OF THE GREATEST PROPHETS TO EARTH, the devil was so terrified that people would heed her message that he hatched a plan to ensure that it would never be heard. He decided to conceal her message as best he could. He looked far and wide for a hiding place that would be so impenetrable, so concealed, that no one would ever hear it. After a long and difficult search the devil finally found the perfect hiding place; he concealed the prophet's message in beauty.

When the prophet finally began her ministry, people would gather around to witness her legendary beauty and elegance. She moved with extraordinary grace, and when she opened her mouth the words sounded as if they had been carefully crafted by some divine poet and sung by a choir of angels. When she spoke, the crowds would reverently murmur, "Isn't she beautiful?"

"How elegantly she moves," "What grace and splendor she has," and "What majestic poetry she crafts."

The great painters would sketch her form, and the poets used her as a muse. The critics would delight themselves in her carefully crafted words, and the sculptors would turn to their marble.

Her message was a difficult one, telling of an impending tragedy that would befall the earth if the people did not learn to love the planet, to live simply, to turn from selfishness and embrace humility. She proclaimed that whole cities would be leveled if people did not learn to love once more without limit, without return, and without borders. But the prophet's cries of condemnation, while celebrated as poetry, were not heard. Her beauty and elegance eclipsed her message, until both she and her words disappeared entirely beneath her voice and form.

So it was that the people moved toward their destruction with dancing and celebration, with eyes that could not see and ears that could not hear.

This story can be understood if we take a moment to consider the opera. It is easy to attend an opera and be so taken in by the audio-visual spectacle that we fail to take note of the message and the story that are housed within it—the message that is more important than the spectacle, the story that gave birth to the performance.

In the same way many of us have been so taken up by what we perceive to be the conceptual splendor of the Bible that we fail to note the message that is housed in the words—the story that cannot possibly be contained or constrained by the words, the message that gave birth to the words.

So then we must be wary of spending all our time poring over the words, talking about them, and memorizing them, for it could well be that such activities could mask the very Word that they bear witness to. Our task is not simply to return to the Bible, but to return to the life-giving Word that gave birth to the Bible and that speaks through it—hearing the message by living it out rather than merely rejoicing in its eloquence.

10

THE PAYOFF

ONCE THERE WAS AN OLD AND LEARNED PRIEST who worked tirelessly in the streets of a city nestled deep in the heart of an empire ruled over by an elderly king. This priest was greatly respected by all the people and would constantly be approached by those who needed help in all manner of issues.

The king of this vast empire had a young son who grew up hating the church. He was disgusted by what he perceived to be its hypocrisy and deception. Because of this deep hatred the young prince would often oversee the imprisonment of church leaders and order the break-up of religious gatherings. But his actions also betrayed a deep jealousy. Indeed he particularly disliked the fact that there was a priest who received the people's respect that he believed was rightly due to him.

Why should the people be so deceived by this old fool? thought the prince. *He is like so many of his type: a coldhearted liar who sells the people lies in order to live.*

The prince harbored a burning desire to put a stop to the priest's work, but he did not want to garner the hatred of the people. So he carefully devised a plan that he believed would expose the hypocrisy of the priest to everyone in the empire once and for all.

He is a poor man, thought the prince. *I will offer him a great sum of money in exchange for a public confession concerning his hypocrisy and the hypocrisy of his church.*

So late one evening, under the cover of darkness, the prince visited the priest and, upon entering his home, said, "I have the power to reach every person in this kingdom through the printed press. For 10,000 rupees would you write a letter to be dispersed throughout the kingdom, in telegrams and newspapers, informing people that you are nothing but a liar and a hypocrite?"

The priest was indeed a poor man who had been born into poverty and had known nothing but need all his life. He thought carefully for a few minutes before finally responding.

"I will do as you ask, but only under three conditions."

"What are your conditions?" replied the prince.

"First, if I do this you must leave me and my church alone."

"Yes," said the prince.

"Second, you must release those brothers and sisters of mine who are innocent of any crime."

"It will be done," replied the prince. "And your third stipulation?"

"Well," said the priest after a great deal of thought, "10,000 rupees is a great deal of money, and I am but a poor man. You will have to give me time to raise it."

■

◆ COMMENTARY   ■

Those who are rich and powerful almost invariably expend great energy insuring that they are seen to be above reproach. While we are all fragile human beings with a multitude of weaknesses, those in power expend a great deal of time and money insuring a public profile that hides this fact, often employing PR organizations dedicated to honing an appropriate image and then publicizing it. These individuals carefully construct a type of ego-ideal, a view of themselves with qualities such as intelligence, kindness, and conviction, which they convince themselves and others is a true reflection of who they really are.

However, the authentic prophet exhibits a different type of leadership. The prophet does not repress the fact that she is weak and prone to temptation, nor does she fear that others will find this out; rather she freely admits to it. Like the apostle Paul, who proclaimed that he was the worst of sinners (1 Timothy 1:15), people of faith will not only have a profound understanding of their own weaknesses but also freely acknowledge them. Instead of seeking to be among the wise, the faithful will admit to their foolishness. For it is through an acknowledgment of our weakness and foolishness that the power and wisdom of faith are expressed. For God chooses the foolish things of the world to shame the wise, and the weak things of the world to expose the impotence of the strong (1 Corinthians 1:27).

In the above story the priest is not afraid of being exposed as weak and unworthy, for he is not interested in building a kingdom in which he is worshiped as king. Rather, the priest wants to point beyond himself, becoming transparent so that what illuminates his life can shine forth without obstacle. Indeed, the priest is so concerned that people would take him as one worthy of worship that when he hears the desire of the prince to expose him as a hypocrite, he takes it as a positive and sincere offer that he must pay for rather than as something that he must be compensated for. Here two incommensurable worlds collide. The power of the prince smashes against the powerlessness of the priest and, in the process, the wisdom of the prince is exposed as hollow in contrast to the depth to be found in the foolishness of the priest.

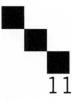

11

FINDING FAITH

THERE WAS ONCE A FIERY PREACHER WHO
POSSESSED A POWERFUL BUT UNUSUAL GIFT.
He found that, from an early age, when he prayed
for individuals, they would supernaturally lose
all of their religious convictions. They would
invariably lose all of their beliefs about the
prophets, the sacred Scriptures, and even God.
So he learned not to pray for people but instead
limited himself to preaching inspiring sermons
and doing good works.

However, one day while traveling across
the country, the preacher found himself in conversation with a businessman who happened to
be going in the same direction. This businessman
was a very powerful and ruthless merchant
banker, one who was honored by his colleagues
and respected by his adversaries.

Their conversation began because the businessman, possessing a deep, abiding faith, had noticed

the preacher reading from the Bible. He introduced himself to the preacher and they began to talk. As they chatted together this powerful man told the preacher all about his faith in God and his love of Christ. He spoke of how his work did not really define who he was but was simply what he had to do.

"The world of business is a cold one," he confided to the preacher, "and in my line of work I find myself in situations that challenge my Christian convictions. But I try, as much as possible, to remain true to my faith. Indeed, I attend a local church every Sunday, participate in a prayer circle, engage in some youth work, and contribute to a weekly Bible study. These activities help to remind me of who I really am."

After listening carefully to the businessman's story, the preacher began to realize the purpose of his unseemly gift. So he turned to the businessman and said, "Would you allow me to pray a blessing into your life?"

The businessman readily agreed, unaware of what would happen. Sure enough, after the preacher had muttered a simple prayer, the man opened his eyes in astonishment.

"What a fool I have been for all these years!" he proclaimed. "It is clear to me now that there is no God above, who is looking out for me, and that there are no sacred texts to guide me, and there is no Spirit to inspire and protect me."

As they parted company the businessman, still confused by what had taken place, returned home. But now that he no longer had any religious beliefs, he began to find it increasingly difficult to continue in his line of work. Faced with the fact that he was now just a hard-nosed businessman working in a corrupt system, rather than a man of God, he began to despise his activity. Within months he had a breakdown, and soon afterward gave up his line of work completely. Feeling better about himself, he then went on to give to the poor all the riches he had accumulated and began to use his considerable managerial expertise to challenge the very system he once participated in, and to help those who had been oppressed by it.

One day, many years later, he happened upon the preacher again while walking through town. He ran over, fell at the preacher's feet, and began to weep with joy. Eventually he looked up at the preacher and smiled, "Thank you, my dear friend, for helping me discover my faith."

◼

◆   COMMENTARY   ◼

In this story we begin to gain an insight into how religious belief can itself be a barrier to living the life of faith. It is all too easy for us to think that our religious beliefs express the deep truth of our inner life while what we do on a daily basis in work is only a mask, a necessary evil that must be endured in order to get by in today's frenetic, consumerist world.

In this way we think that it is our commitment to prayer groups, church meetings, and Bible studies that reflects the essence of our inner lives. Our religious groups on the weekends and in the evenings are thought to be sites of resistance that provide us with the strength to question our world and avoid getting fully caught up in it.

However, could it be that these activities are in fact the very things that allow us to fully engage with the world? What if we need our prayer groups and Bible studies because they act as a type of safety valve that actually allows us to release the tensions and stresses of our work so that, the next day, we can return again? If this is so, then the activities that we think critique the unjust world are really the very activities that this world requires in order to run smoothly. Our church activities are then nothing more than a type of air vent in the machine.

This logic is beautifully expressed in *The Matrix Trilogy*, directed by the Wachowski Brothers. In the first film we learn that there is a city where people are free from the AI prison where the majority of humans are held and that Neo (Keanu Reeves) is the hero who can bring freedom. However, in the later films we learn that there have been many cities before Zion (the free city) and that Neo is just the latest in a long line of messiah-like individuals who have risen up to challenge the machines.

Furthermore, we learn that the machines are actually behind what initially seems to be the very force that would threaten them: they are behind the development of Zion and they provide the necessary conditions for Neo (and the other freedom fighters) to arise. Why? Because they understand that, for the oppressive system they have constructed to work, the Matrix needs to include a site of resistance.

In daily life there are reams of activities that are publicly disavowed by the government and society at large, yet are privately permitted. Among these are turning a blind eye to prostitution in certain areas, and the fact that we can all go ten miles per hour over the speed limit without too much fear of getting fined. These acts allow people to disobey the law in ways that are actually unofficially sanctioned by the law. We who engage in such state-sanctioned transgressions are otherwise good law-abiding citizens. Indeed, our ability to break the law in small ways is part of what keeps us law-abiding the rest of the time. If we were not able to engage in small acts of transgression, if the law were absolutely unbending, then we would begin to rebel against it in a fundamental way. By creating leniency within the law, the law is not experienced as oppressive and is thus more likely to be accepted with all its flaws.

In the above story I attempt to explore and critique this problem by putting into fictional form the insights of the theologian Dietrich

Bonhoeffer in *Letters and Papers from Prison*. Here Bonhoeffer rejected religion because he felt that it places God on the outer edges of life as the answer to our current ignorance (for example, as the name we give to the one who created the world) or as the one we turn to in the private sphere (such as at church and in the home). Bonhoeffer rejected this and refused to give God a place in the world, because when God is given a place, God is confined to a specific location (and that location is usually on the edges of life). Instead he advocated an existence fully immersed in the world, utterly taken up by the concerns of the world, one that pours itself out in the joys and sufferings of the world.

Such a move could of course be misunderstood as a way of actively denying God. It could be described as a humanism in which people are encouraged to take responsibility for their own lives rather than looking for some divine answer. Yet for Bonhoeffer this was not the end of the story. If religion gives God a place, and humanism denies that place, then he claimed that Christianity fully embraces this humanism, not as a way of denying God, but as the way of fully affirming God—denying God a place so that God is affirmed in every place. Here one fully lives in the world as a way of fully living before God. Hence he wrote, "Before God and with God we live without God."[1]

The result of such thinking is the affirmation of a faith that permeates all our actions rather than being exhibited only when faced with something we cannot understand, or at some prayer meeting, or in some weekly service to the poor. Such an expression thus strikes against the very roots of inauthentic resistance and demands a truly radical reconfiguring of our social existence.

To put this in religious language, the above story asks if perhaps the devil, far from hating our multitude of church activities, positively loves them, for it is in these very activities that we are able to become such productive agents in carrying out his insidious desires—making changes in the world that fundamentally ensure everything in the world remains the same.

PART TWO

G-O-D-I-S-N-O-W-H-E-R-E ■

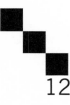

12

BEING THE RESURRECTION

LATE THAT EVENING A GROUP OF UNKNOWN DISCIPLES PACKED THEIR FEW BELONGINGS AND LEFT FOR A DISTANT SHORE, for they could not bear to stay another moment in the place where their Messiah had just been crucified. Weighed down with sorrow, they left that place, never to return. Instead they traveled a great distance in search of a land that they could call home. After months of difficult travel, they finally happened upon an isolated area that was ideal for setting up a new community. Here they found fertile ground, clean water, and a nearby forest from which to harvest material needed to build shelter. So they settled there, founding a community far from Jerusalem, a community where they vowed to keep the memory of Christ alive and live in simplicity, love, and forgiveness, just as he had taught them.

The members of this community lived in great solitude for over a hundred years, spending their days reflecting on the life of Jesus and attempting to remain faithful to his ways. And they did all this despite the overwhelming sorrow in their heart.

But their isolation was eventually broken when, early one morning, a small band of missionaries reached the settlement. These missionaries were amazed at the community they found. What was most startling to them was that these people had no knowledge of the resurrection and the ascension of Christ, for they had left Jerusalem before his return from the dead on the third day. Without hesitation, the missionaries gathered together all the community members and recounted what had occurred after the imprisonment and bloody crucifixion of their Lord.

That evening there was a great festival in the camp as people celebrated the news of the missionaries. Yet, as the night progressed, one of the missionaries noticed that the leader of the community was absent. This bothered the young man, so he set out to look for this respected elder. Eventually he found the community's leader crouched low in a small hut on the fringe of the village, praying and weeping.

"Why are you in such sorrow?" asked the missionary in amazement. "Today is a time for great celebration."

"It may indeed be a day for great celebration, but this is also a day of sorrow," replied the elder, who remained crouched on the floor. "Since the founding of this community we have followed the ways taught to us by Christ. We pursued his ways faithfully even though it cost us dearly, and we remained resolute despite the belief that death had defeated him and would one day defeat us also."

The elder slowly got to his feet and looked the missionary compassionately in the eyes.

"Each day we have forsaken our very lives for him because we judged him wholly worthy of the sacrifice, wholly worthy of our being. But now, following your news, I am concerned that my children and my children's children may follow him, not because of his radical life and supreme sacrifice, but selfishly, because his sacrifice will ensure their personal salvation and eternal life."

With this the elder turned and left the hut, making his way to the celebrations that could be heard dimly in the distance, leaving the missionary crouched on the floor.

■

COMMENTARY   ■

This story was written in order to explore what it means for a person to affirm the resurrection of Christ. While the community described above knew nothing of the literal Resurrection, there is a sense in which they affirmed the reality of the Resurrection in a more radical way than many of those who confess such a belief. The reason for this relates to the fact that, for many today, belief in the Resurrection simply acts as a guarantee of eternal life and cosmic meaning. In this way, the belief itself is divorced from action and acts as nothing more than a type of divine insurance policy. In contrast, this tale asks whether Resurrection is fundamentally something that is lived and does not depend on one's subjective belief.

In order to explore this theme the story creates a type of prolonged Holy Saturday experience. (Holy Saturday refers to the day that is nestled between Good Friday and Easter Sunday.) In this liminal space between witnessing the Crucifixion and hearing of the Resurrection, the members of the community described above have given themselves wholly to the teachings of Christ. In this way, they follow him without thought of some future reward, and thus they follow him in a truly sacrificial way.

It is in this dedicated commitment to Christ that one can say that the Resurrection is truly made manifest, for while there is no intellectual affirmation of Christ's living presence, there is an incarnated testimony to this presence. Here Jesus is testified to as present in the life and actions of the community. This affirmation is not wrapped up in some abstract belief; it is testified to in the texture of their lives.

Not only does this cause us to rethink the necessity of believing in the Resurrection, it can actually cause us to wonder whether this belief could sometimes act as a barrier to really affirming its reality. As mentioned above, it is not uncommon to find people within the church who believe for self-interested reasons—for example, affirming Christianity out of a desire to enter heaven.

When confronted with this, is not the Christian obliged to undermine the intellectual belief in Resurrection—inviting the person to reflect upon the life and death of Christ in and of themselves? Far from being an unorthodox idea, this is precisely what happens in the Christian calendar every year during Tenebrae.

We can even see in the Gospels this idea of an orthodox theological belief getting in the way of its true meaning. For instance, Jesus warned Simon Peter against revealing his identity to others. In the Gospel according to Matthew we read,

> When Jesus came to the region of Caesarea Philippi, he asked his disciples, "Who do people say the Son of Man is?"
>
> They replied, "Some say John the Baptist; others say Elijah; and still others, Jeremiah or one of the prophets."
>
> "But what about you?" he asked. "Who do you say I am?"
>
> Simon Peter answered, "You are the Christ, the Son of the living God."
>
> Jesus replied, "Blessed are you, Simon son of Jonah, for this was not revealed to you

by man, but by my Father in heaven. And I tell you that you are Peter, and on this rock I will build my church, and the gates of Hades will not overcome it. I will give you the keys of the kingdom of heaven; whatever you bind on earth will be bound in heaven, and whatever you loose on earth will be loosed in heaven." *Then he warned his disciples not to tell anyone that he was the Christ.*
(Matthew 16:13–20, italics mine)

Unlike today, when many people wish to proclaim from rooftops that Jesus is Messiah, Jesus is recorded here as wishing to keep his identity a secret, almost as if such an idea could actually get in the way of what he stood for.

We can understand this when we grasp how affirming Christ as the Messiah is not a verbal act but rather is testified to through one's life. Is this not how we ought to read the statement, "Therefore I tell you that no one who is speaking by the Spirit of God says, 'Jesus be cursed,' and no one can say, 'Jesus is Lord,' except by the Holy Spirit" (1 Corinthians 12:3)? Of course this does not mean that one is unable to say the words *Jesus is Lord* except by the Spirit of God. The point is that the affirmation "Jesus is Lord" is not some disembodied intellectual claim. It is an incarnated affirmation declared in the life of those who pour themselves out for the poor, the oppressed, and the enemy.

This story thus explores the controversial possibility that Christians are not called to believe in the Resurrection but rather are called to be the site where Resurrection takes place—the site where Christ's presence is testified to in action.

13

THE PRODIGAL FATHER

THERE WAS ONCE A RICH AND KINDLY FATHER who lived with his two sons in a lavish mansion. But late one evening, in the very dead of night, the father packed a few small items and left quietly.

The first son awoke the next day and, upon discovering his father's disappearance, continued with his chores religiously. Days passed into months, and these months gradually dissolved into years. Through toil and rationalization, this son successfully repressed the haunting fact that the father had abandoned them. Instead of facing the pain, he allowed the reality of the situation to fester silently in the depth of his being.

The other son also refused to face up to the pain of his father's midnight exodus. In confusion and fear he withdrew his share of the father's inheritance and ran away, losing himself in worldly distractions of all kinds. But he found that no matter where he traveled, he could not escape the sorrow in his heart, and no matter what activity he engaged in, the amnesia it offered was not enough to cloud the memory of his father's disappearance. In addition to this, he soon found himself utterly destitute and poor. After only a few years he found himself without money or friends, working on a pig farm, where he would have to share the scraps that he fed to the animals in order to supplement his diet.

After many months of this pitiful existence, he decided to face up to his father's disappearance and return home.

When he finally reached the great mansion, he found his brother still caring for the property, still toiling on the land, and still suppressing the memory of their father's exodus. The brother who had never left held resentment in his heart against the one who had squandered his inheritance only to return empty-handed. However, the other brother paid no heed to this animosity, for his gaze was set upon a deeper concern. Each day he would carefully ready a calf for slaughter and lay out his father's favorite cloak in preparation for a great feast of celebration. Once he had done this he would then sit by the entrance of the mansion and passionately await the father's return.

He waits there still, to this very day, yearning for the homecoming of the prodigal father with longing and forgiveness in his heart.

COMMENTARY

This story was originally written on a scrap of paper while I was attending a Quaker meeting. As I sat in silence that Sunday morning, it felt as if I were in the presence of people who were faithfully waiting for God to show up. Indeed, on that dark and cold Sunday morning it seemed as if those gathered were prepared to wait their entire lives for God if that was what it would take. As I thought about this, my mind wandered to the prodigal son story, in which God is portrayed as waiting for the return of His wayward offspring. But being among this small band of believers, I began to wonder what form the story would take if written from a human perspective, from the perspective of those who remain faithful to God yet who feel that God is distant. The story thus became a personal reflection on the theme of divine withdrawal.

Reflections on the idea of God's withdrawal span the Christian tradition and have been baptized with many names, such as the "dark night of the soul" or the "cloud of unknowing." That tradition was poignantly mined in much of the theology that emanated from those who experienced the horror of the death camps during the Second World War.

Many theologians have pointed out that God, by God's very nature, always transcends our grasp and so will always be experienced as withdrawn from our understanding and experience. This view seeks to respect the wonder and majesty of the divine, and draw out how God's presence is never full presence, not simply because of our limits, but because of God's uncontainable nature.

Yet, there is another sense in which believers have reflected on the theme of God's withdrawal, one that has nothing to do with the nature of God as transcendent but rather with the sense that God has abandoned us. We see this theme poignantly expressed by Christ on the cross when he cries out, "My God, my God, why have you forsaken me?" The absence of God as testified to in this prayer is not the result of God's being perceived as transcendent, but rather derives from the sense of God's withdrawing from us in our hour of need.

It was this latter experience I had in mind as I wrote the above story. For I was intrigued by how remaining faithful to God in the midst of God's seeming infidelity to us is actually a deep and unique aspect of the Judeo-Christian tradition, one that spans the entire biblical text, from Genesis to Revelation.

From the angry accusations of the psalmist to Christ's anguished cry from the cross, such prayers are not condemned by the text but celebrated. In these broken prayers we find a singular depth of commitment, intimacy, and struggle. For these accusations of abandonment address God directly and thus affirm a resolute longing for God in the very expression of their loneliness.

14

AWAITING THE MESSIAH

THERE IS AN ANCIENT STORY THAT SPEAKS OF A SECOND COMING OF THE MESSIAH. It is said that he arrived anonymously one dull Monday morning at the gates of a great city to go about his Father's business.

There was much for him to do. While many years had passed since his last visit, the same suffering was present all around. Still there were the poor, the sick, and the oppressed. Still there were the outcasts, and still there were the righteous who pitied them, and the authorities who exploited them.

For a long time no one took any notice of this desert wanderer with his weather-beaten face and ragged, dusty clothes—this quiet man who spent his time living among the sick and unwanted. The great city labored on like a mammoth beast, ignorant of the one who dwelt within its bowels.

The story goes that the Messiah eventually decided to reveal his identity to a chosen few who had remained faithful to his teachings. These people met together in a tiny, unknown church on the outskirts of the city to pray and to serve the poor.

As the Messiah entered the modest sanctuary one Sunday morning, his eyes fell upon the tiny group huddled in the corner, each one praying and weeping for the day of the Lord. As they prayed, those who had gathered in the church slowly began to feel the gaze of Christ penetrate their souls. Silence began to descend within the circle as they realized who had entered their sacred home. For a time no one dared to speak. Then the leader of the group gathered her courage, approached Christ, fell at his feet, and cried, "We have waited so long for your return. For so many years we have waited patiently for you to come. Today, as with every other day, we prayed passionately for your arrival."

Then she stood up and looked Christ in the eyes:

"Now that you are with us we have but one question."

Christ listened, knowing already what it would be.

"Tell us, Christ, *when will you arrive?*"

The Messiah did not answer but simply smiled. Then he joined the others in their prayers and tears. He remains there still, to this very day, waiting, watching, and serving in that tiny, unknown church on the outskirts of the city.

■

COMMENTARY   ■

This story was directly inspired by a short reflection from the enigmatic work of Maurice Blanchot in *The Writing of the Disaster.*[2] So how should we approach this story? In many ways it questions our commonsense understanding of what it means for someone to be with us. We often think that desire arises insofar as what we desire is absent. But what if we have got this all wrong, at least in relation to God and other humans? What if we can long for the arrival of someone only when that person has turned up? What if we can desire only the one we are already in relationship with? What if the presence of the other is precisely that which makes us yearn for that person?

In order to grasp this possibility we must take a moment to imagine that we are single and are desiring a relationship with someone. We may, for example, desire a relationship because we are lonely or because we feel incomplete without another person. The point is that we are seeking a relationship with *some*one. We cannot at this point seek the arrival of a particular person, insomuch as we have not yet met a particular person to whom we are attracted. We desire someone, but that someone is no one in particular. This person is nothing more than an idea, an image that we have in our mind. Now imagine that one day we meet a person and begin to develop a relationship. At this point, our desire for someone is transformed into a desire for the person with whom we are developing a relationship. We no longer desire someone in abstraction, we desire a specific person. We could not have desired this person before we met them, because we did not know them.

When we meet our beloved we will often feel that we were always looking for that person, that we were always incomplete without them. However, this "always" must be understood as a retroactive creation, something that happens after the fact. The lover is the one whose heart proclaims, "I had no need of you until I met you, but now I know I always needed you." Or alternatively, "I had no desire for you until I met you, and now I know that I have always desired you."

The point here is that our desire is not satisfied by the arrival of our beloved but rather born there. But not only is it born there, the presence of our beloved sustains our desire. The reason for this relates to the fact that we only ever know our beloved in part, as if through a glass darkly. Their incoming testifies to a simultaneous withdrawal.

The television program *Dr. Who* may help us to understand this structure. In the series the doctor travels through time and space in a TARDIS. From the outside the TARDIS appears as a small box in the shape of a telephone booth. However, on the inside it has seemingly infinite proportions. In a similar way, is not the small, fragile exterior frame of our beloved not experienced as housing an interior world of infinite proportions? It is because of this that our encounter with someone does not equal some kind of full contact with them. People we have known all of our life will remain a mystery to us as much as they will remain a mystery to themselves. Indeed, it is often only as a relationship develops that one begins to realize the depth of mystery that the other person's fragile physical frame houses. At the beginning of a relationship, one may often have the intoxicating feeling that one knows his or her partner intimately and completely. It can take many years to come to appreciate and respect the impenetrable mystery that our beloved really is.

Therefore, when the one we love arrives, we experience this person simultaneously as one who is still to come, not despite their presence but *because* of it. The presence of our beloved testifies to our beloved's absence, to the fact that our beloved is also still distant from us. This understanding can help us appreciate ideas such as the kingdom of God being both now and not yet and of the revelation of Jesus always being a type of concealment.

The incoming of God as expressed in the incarnation represents a beautiful expression of this simultaneous revealing and withdrawal, for in the Incarnation the mystery of God is not dissipated but rather deepened. The mystery is not unmasked, but rather dwells with us, in our midst. The mystery is thus not overcome in the Incarnation but rather encountered there.

15

THE LAST TRIAL

YOU SIT IN SILENCE CONTEMPLATING WHAT HAS JUST TAKEN PLACE. Only moments ago you were alive and well, relaxing at home with friends. Then there was a deep, crushing pain in your chest that brought you crashing to the floor. The pain has now gone, but you are no longer in your home. Instead, you find yourself standing on the other side of death waiting to stand before the judgment seat and discover where you will spend eternity. As you reflect upon your life your name is called, and you are led down a long corridor into a majestic sanctuary with a throne located in its center. Sitting on this throne is a huge, breathtaking being who looks up at you and begins to speak.

"My name is Lucifer, and I am the angel of light."

You are immediately filled with fear and trembling as you realize that you are face to face with the enemy of all that is true and good. Then the angel continues: "I have cast God down from his throne and banished Christ to the realm of eternal death. It is I who hold the keys to the kingdom. It is I who am the gatekeeper of paradise, and it is for me alone to decide who shall enter eternal joy and who shall be forsaken."

After saying these words, he sits up and stretches out his vast arms. "In my right hand I hold eternal life and in my left hand eternal death. Those who would bow down and acknowledge me as their god shall pass through the gates of paradise and experience an eternity of bliss, but all those who refuse will be vanquished to the second death with their Christ."

After a long pause he bends toward you and speaks, "Which will you choose?"

■

COMMENTARY   ■

In a similar manner to the ancient myths of Greece, a story such as this offers the reader a type of thought experiment in which one can place two seemingly inseparable ideas in opposition to one another in order to explore a particular theme.

In positing this thought experiment, the believer is invited to ask whether faith is focused on external rewards or whether it is embraced as its own reward. This story can thus help us contemplate what the true wealth of faith really consists of. For if our encounter with the source of our faith *is* the treasure that Christianity offers (rather than that which can lead to treasure) then it does not matter what results from my embracing of this faith. In this way the believer, when faced with the above situation, would be able to stand defiant against the devil and enter death with Christ rather than entering heaven alone.

16

SINS OF THE FATHER

ON JUDGMENT DAY A GREAT SUMMONS WENT FORTH TO THE SEA, commanding that she give up her dead, and a voice called out to Hades demanding that the prisoners be released from their chains. Then the angels gathered up the whole of humanity and brought the masses to the great white throne of God. The noise was deafening, but when a mighty angel stood up and opened the great book of judgment, all living things fell silent.

The first to be judged stood up and approached the angel who held this great text. Once the accused entered the dock, all humanity rose up and spoke as one: "When we were hungry you gave us nothing to eat. When we were thirsty, you gave us nothing to drink. We were strangers and you did not invite us in. We needed clothes and you did not clothe us. We were sick and in prison and you did not look after us."

Once the accusation had been heard, silence once more descended upon all of creation. They had pronounced their judgment on God and now waited to hear God's defense.

COMMENTARY

Within the biblical text there are numerous instances of human beings standing forward to accuse God of injustice. For example, we read of Jeremiah crying out,

> Why is my pain unending
> and my wound grievous and incurable?
> Will you be to me like a deceptive brook,
>   like a spring that fails?
>
> (Jeremiah 15:18)

Elsewhere in the Old Testament we read of Job turning toward heaven and shouting,

> Am I the sea, or the monster of the deep,
>   that you put me under guard?
> When I think my bed will comfort me
>   and my couch will ease my complaint,

even then you frighten me with dreams
       and terrify me with visions,
so that I prefer strangling and death,
       rather than this body of mine.
I despise my life; I would not live forever.
       Let me alone; my days have no meaning.
What is man that you make so much of him,
       that you give him so much attention,
that you examine him every morning
       and test him every moment?
Will you never look away from me,
       or let me alone even for an instant?
If I have sinned, what have I done to you,
       O watcher of men?
Why have you made me your target?
       Have I become a burden to you?
Why do you not pardon my offenses
       and forgive my sins?
For I will soon lie down in the dust;
       you will search for me, but I will be
       no more.

                              (Job 7:12–21)

Far from being something to condemn or
discourage, the idea of fighting with God as

part of what it means to express one's deep and abiding faith in God seems to be a unique aspect of the Judeo-Christian tradition. Is this not the lesson we receive when we read in Genesis that God blesses Jacob with the name *Israel*, a name earned by Jacob because he had ferociously fought with God and overcome? This word is more than a name for one individual; it comes to represent a whole people: a people who would show their faithfulness and religiosity through a passionate, often uneasy, interaction with God. These people were prepared to wrestle with, disagree with, and even accuse their creator. Indeed this idea seems to permeate the whole Bible. We witness this wrestling from the book of Genesis, when we read of the fight between Jacob and God, right through to Revelation, where we read that God condemns the church of Laodicea saying, "I know your deeds, that you are neither cold nor hot. I wish you were either one or the other! So, because you are lukewarm—neither hot nor cold—I am about to spit you out of my mouth" (Revelation 3:15–16).

17

THE ORTHODOX HERETIC

THERE WAS ONCE A SMALL TOWN FILLED WITH BELIEVERS WHO ALWAYS SOUGHT TO ACT IN OBEDIENCE to the teachings of God. When faced with difficult situations the leaders of the community would often be found deep in prayer, or searching the Scriptures, for guidance and wisdom. Late one evening, in the middle of winter, a young man from the neighboring city arrived at the gates of the town's church seeking refuge. The caretaker, a man of deep faith, immediately let him in and, seeing that he was hungry and cold, provided a warm meal and some fresh clothes.

After he had rested the young man explained how he had fled the city because the authorities had labeled him a political dissident. It turned out that the man had been critical of both the government and the church in his work as a journalist. The caretaker brought the young man back to his home and allowed him to stay until a plan had been worked out concerning what to do next.

When the priest was informed of what had happened, he called the leaders of the town together in order to work out what ought to be done. After two days of discussion it was agreed that the man should be handed over to the authorities in order to face up to the crimes he had committed. But the caretaker protested, saying, "This man has committed no crimes, he has merely criticized what he believes to be the injustices perpetrated by authorities in the name of God."

"What you say may be true," replied the priest, "but his presence puts the whole of this town in danger, for what if the authorities find out where he is and learn that we have protected him?"

But the caretaker refused to hand him over to the priest, saying, "He is my guest, and while he is under my roof I will ensure that no harm comes to him. If you take him from me by force, then I will publicly attest to having helped him and suffer the same injustice as my guest."

The caretaker was well loved by the people, and the priest had no intention of letting something happen to him. So the leaders went away again and this time searched the Scriptures for an answer, for they knew that the caretaker was a man of deep faith. After a whole night of poring over the Scriptures, the leaders came back to the caretaker saying, "We have read the sacred book all through the night seeking guidance and have found that it tells us that we must respect the authorities of this land and witness to the truth of faith through submission to them."

But the caretaker also knew the sacred words of Scripture and told them that the Bible also asked that we care for those who suffer and are persecuted.

So there and then, in desperation the leaders began to pray fervently. They beseeched God to speak to them, not as a still, small voice in their conscience, but rather in the way that he had spoken to Abraham and Moses. They begged God to communicate directly to them so that the caretaker would see the error of his ways. Sure enough, the sky began to darken, and God descended from heaven, saying, "The priest and elders speak the truth, my friend. In order to protect the town this man must be handed over to the authorities."

But the caretaker, a man of deep faith, looked up to heaven and replied, "If you want me to remain faithful to you, my God, then I can do nothing but refuse your advice. For I do not need the Scriptures or your words to tell me what I ought to do. You have already demanded that I look after this man. You have already written that I must protect him at all costs. Your words of love have been spelled out by the lines of this man's face, your text is found in the texture of his flesh. So, my God, I defy you precisely in order to remain faithful to you."

With this, God turned to the town's leaders and addressed them directly: "If I cannot convince him, then neither will you. Now leave him in peace." Then God smiled and quietly withdrew, knowing that the matter had finally been settled.

COMMENTARY

This story was partly inspired by an old Jewish legend in which God mourns over the way that his people are acting. In tears God says to the angels, "My children remember me but forget my ways.

How I wish they would forget about me and keep my ways." The key to understanding this idea lies in the notion that God is affirmed in, and only in, acts of love—not a love that loves only those who love back, but a love that embraces the stranger, the outsider, the enemy.

We can see a similar idea being played out in the story of God's destruction of Sodom. In Genesis we read that God is contemplating whether or not to destroy Sodom because of its immorality. It is interesting that the writer portrays God as doing this in such a way that Abraham overhears. The next part of the story involves Abraham arguing directly with God about this destruction, and causing God to reconsider (see Genesis 18:20–21). God at first is thinking of destroying the city because of the quantity of sin, but Abraham causes God to take into consideration the innocent who would also be harmed. What we learn here is that there is a Biblical injunction to question authority, regardless of who or what that authority is, when we believe that authority is not defending the persecuted. For in the Bible the face of a helpless, suffering child has a greater call on us than any institution or heavenly voice.

It is in the face of the suffering child or the flesh of a tortured man that the ethical demand of God is written.

For this reason we can embrace Christianity as that which is lived wholly in the world, as that which finds God in the act of giving to those in need and receiving from others as we are in need. We can approach Christianity as a grounded faith, rooted firmly in the soil of the world. It is as we live fully in the world, taking total responsibility for our actions, that we demonstrate our faith.

This approach fully embraces the idea that Christ is found in our interaction with others, in our offering food to the hungry and water to the thirsty. This is an incarnational approach that hears God's call emanating from the very heart of the world rather than as entering it from outside.

18

THE MISSION OF JUDAS

EARLY ONE EVENING, WHILE THE OTHER DISCIPLES WERE BUSY PREPARING FOR THE UPCOMING FEAST OF UNLEAVENED BREAD, Judas fell into a deep and troubled sleep. While he lay motionless on the hard ground, he received a terrifying vision.

In this vision, Judas found himself around a table with the other disciples, sharing an intimate Passover meal with Jesus. At this meal, Jesus spoke solemnly about broken flesh and sacrificial blood while breaking bread and pouring wine. Judas was then transported to the local Jewish temple, where he promised to identify Jesus with a kiss so that the religious authorities could arrest him.

In the blink of an eye, he found himself in the Garden of Gethsemane, embracing Jesus and tenderly kissing him on the cheek. This was followed swiftly by the arrest, trial, torture, and death of his Lord.

Yet the dream did not end there; instead Judas went on to experience his own sorrow and remorse at this act of betrayal and see firsthand his own harrowing suicide. As if this were not enough, he then found himself in a courtroom with disciples through the ages condemning his actions and pouring out insults.

Yet in this vision he went on to witness the Resurrection and the Ascension of his Beloved. He saw the spread of Jesus' message across the entire world, its victory over the forces of Rome and the way in which it would transform the lives of countless millions. When Judas awoke in a cold sweat from this nightmare, he recalled a teaching that had recently been given by Jesus. Only yesterday Jesus had addressed his disciples, saying, "The hour has come for the Son of Man to be glorified. I tell you the truth, unless a kernel of wheat falls to the ground and dies, it remains only a single seed. But if it dies, it produces many seeds. The man who loves his life will lose it, while the man who hates his life in this world will keep it for eternal life" (John 12:23–25).

As Judas reflected again on these words and on the vision he had just experienced, he felt a profound sadness well up within his heart, for he finally knew why he had been called. He knew what needed to be done. He understood now what his destiny was.

COMMENTARY

In this story a fictitious scenario is created that casts the betrayal of Judas in an entirely different light. Here we are led to conceive of Judas as one of the most courageous figures in the Bible, as one who betrayed Christ, not because of a love for money or because he had been overpowered by some demonic influence, but rather because he knew what would result from that betrayal.

While this is a fictitious narrative, the idea of playing with the story in this way is encouraged by the biblical text itself. The various conflicting references to Judas invite us to imagine and explore different motives for his behavior (something I explore in my book *The Fidelity of Betrayal*). The various accounts found in the Gospels cause us to ask whether Judas betrayed Jesus (handing him over for money), whether Jesus betrayed Judas (employing him as a disposable pawn in a divine strategy), or whether Judas and Jesus worked together (planning in advance what was to take place).

This latter possibility is suggested most strongly in the Gospel of Mark, when a woman approaches Jesus and pours expensive perfume over his body. When the disciples question the appropriateness of this act, Jesus responds by pointing out that she is doing it to prepare his body for burial. At this moment, Judas leaves the room and meets with the religious authorities. What we are left wondering is how the woman knew to pour the perfume over his body, why Jesus knew that she was preparing his body for burial, and why this ritual acted as the sign for Judas to approach the religious authorities. One is left asking whether these three people had met up previously and carefully planned what would take place.

By understanding the complexity of the betrayal, we are led to consider whether certain acts that might appear to be fundamentally against God could actually be gestures of fidelity to God.

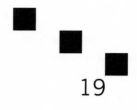

19

THE AGNOSTIC
WHO BECAME AN ATHEIST

THERE WAS ONCE A WORLD-RENOWNED PHILOSOPHER WHO, from an early age, set himself the task of proving once and for all the nonexistence of God. Of course, such a task was immense, for the various arguments for and against the existence of God had done battle over the ages without either being able to claim victory.

He was, however, a genius without equal, and he possessed a singular vision that drove him to work each day and long into every night in order to understand the intricacies of every debate, every discussion, and every significant work on the subject.

The philosopher's project began to earn him respect among his fellow professors when, as a young man, he published the first volume of what would turn out to be a finely honed, painstakingly researched, encyclopedic masterpiece on the subject of God. The first volume of this work argued persuasively that the various ideas of God that had been expressed throughout antiquity were philosophically incoherent and logically flawed. As each new volume appeared, he offered, time and again, devastating critiques of the theological ideas that had been propagated through different periods of history. In his early forties, he completed the last volume, which brought him up to the present day.

However, the completion of this work did not satisfy him. He still had not found a convincing argument that would demonstrate once and for all the nonexistence of God. For all he had shown was that all the notions of God up to that time had been problematic.

So he spent another sixteen years researching arguments and interrogating them with a highly nuanced, logical analysis. But by now he was in his late fifties and had slowly begun to despair of ever completing his life project.

Then, late one evening while he was locked away in his study, bent wearily over his old oak desk, surrounded by a vast sea of books, he felt a deep stillness descend upon the room. As he sat there motionless, everything around him seemed to radiate an inexpressible light and warmth. Then, deep in his heart he heard the voice of God address him:

"Dear friend, the task you have set yourself is a futile one. I have watched all these years as you poured your being into this endless task. Yet, you fail to understand that your project can be brought to completion only with my help. Your dedication and single-mindedness have not gone unnoticed, and they have won my respect. As a result, I will tell you a sacred secret meant only for a few. . . . Dear friend, *I do not exist.*"

Then, all of a sudden, everything appeared as it was before, and the philosopher was left sitting at his desk with a deep smile breaking across his face. He put his pen away and left his study, never to return. Instead, in gratitude to God for helping him complete his lifelong project, he dedicated his remaining years to serving the poor.

COMMENTARY

The word *theism* refers to belief in God, while *atheism* refers to the rejection of this belief. However, just as belief in God is always a belief in a certain concept of God, so the rejection of God is always the rejection of one or more concepts of God. In the same way that one can ask a theist, "What God do you believe in?" so one can ask an atheist, "What God do you not believe in?" Traditional atheism is always regional in nature, for it limits itself to attacking some particular conception or conceptions of God. Concrete expressions of atheism are regional, not only because there are so many conceptions of God in existence today, but also because there are an infinite number of possible conceptions that have yet to be dreamed of. While one form of atheism may question one form of theism, it will not necessarily have anything to say concerning a different form. Therefore, atheism, at its best, is always provisional—meaning that it is always limited to a particular expression of belief.

Because of this, the philosopher in the above story struggled to find an atheism that would be able to reject all possible conceptions of God. Only when God showed up was the philosopher finally able to attain a truly universal atheism, one that could reject, in advance, any conceptual description of God. The reason for this lies in the idea that God utterly transcends all concepts and thus cannot be approached as an object at all.

It is common for those who argue for and against the existence of God to assume that the word *God* is used by believers to refer to something that we can point toward, distance ourselves from, and dispassionately reflect upon. However, one can reject this idea of God as nothing but a form of idolatry that is opposed to the biblical expression of God. This approach questions any expression that would reduce God to the realm of objects. Here no theistic rendering of God is allowed to lay claim to God, for God dwells above and beyond all names. God is rather approached as the ineffable source that is received but never conceived. God is thus not approached as an object, but rather encountered as an absolute subject who transforms our relationship with all objects. Just as the light in the room cannot be seen but rather allows us to see, so God is not directly experienced but rather is the name we give to a whole new way of experiencing. Is this not how we are to approach the idea of being born again? One does not experience birth; rather, birth is what opens us up to the world of experience. Hence, religious experience is not really experience as such but the opening into a different way of experiencing.

Because every description of God testified to in the Judeo-Christian tradition falls short, the encounter with this God is the very event that opens up a universal atheism. In other words, only an atheism that proclaims no concept of God (theism) can do justice to the reality of God. In this way, all concepts of God are now rejected *in advance*.

Religious believers can therefore affirm atheism in the most radical sense because they refuse to let any conception of God take the place of God. The thoughtful believer is not questioning or denying the value or importance of positive descriptions (theism), but simply refusing to let those provisional, fractured descriptions take on the guise of absolute authority. For what gives birth to the believer stands before all descriptions and remains free from them.

Thus a philosophically coherent atheism can be described as a profoundly Judeo-Christian position, for it is a position that refuses to let any description colonize the source that we call God, a source that stands outside temporal duration and spatial location. Once we understand this, we can stop arguing about God and, like the philosopher in the above story, dedicate our lives to being the manifestation of God.

20

GOD JOINS THE ARMY

MANY CENTURIES AGO AN INDEPENDENT ISLAND WAS ATTACKED BY THE DICTATOR OF A NEARBY NATION, a nation with vast resources and a mighty army. Upon landing on the island, this army moved with little resistance toward the capital city. With less than a day to decide what action to take, the leaders of the island desperately discussed what could be done in the face of the encroaching army. They were hugely outnumbered, out-resourced, and out-skilled, so defeat seemed inevitable.

The leaders never made a decision without first consulting with their religious oracle, so they approached her small dwelling on the edge of the city. The oracle was a woman who possessed great insight and had the ability to see into realms usually reserved only for the angels. Upon hearing about the invasion, she spent an entire day in deep meditation before finally coming to the leaders with a heavy heart, saying,

"I bring sad news: I have been told that God himself has joined with our enemies and has put all of his power at their disposal."

This ominous message sent deep fear and trembling through the hearts of the elders. In response one proclaimed, "We must surrender now and pray that they will have mercy on us." Then another responded, "No, let us make ready our fastest ships and set sail with as many people as we can. Perhaps we can sneak past their navy while it is dark." But the chief, a strong man with deep faith, remained calm throughout the debate. At the end of the discussion he said, "Please trust me, I know what to do in order to ensure that we make it through this dark hour."

The chief was well respected by all, and so, in the absence of a plan, they reluctantly agreed to trust him.

That day he called together all the men of the city who could fight. He then sent those with young children home, followed by those who had been married for less than a year. By the end of this process the remaining men numbered less than a few thousand, a tiny group in comparison to the army they would soon face.

These brave men were then armed and told to march behind their chief toward the encroaching army. That day there was a bloody battle and many tragically lost their lives. But, to everyone's utter surprise, by the end of the day the dictator's seemingly impenetrable army had been dealt a devastating blow and had turned away in retreat.

The entire island was dumbstruck as they heard of how the enemy had run in fear and trembling back to their homeland. The oracle however was more confused than most, for she knew what had been kept secret from the people: that God had joined the side of the enemy and put all his vast power at their disposal. So the oracle approached the chief and said, "How did you know to fight when the odds where impossibly high and when you knew that God himself was pitted against you?"

But the chief merely smiled and replied, "Surely you know that it does not matter which side God is on. When God is involved, the oppressed always win."

COMMENTARY

While this tale may at first seem rather strange, we must remember that this is not the first time that God has been defeated in a fight. For example, Jacob is said to have grappled with God all night and overcome. The leader of the island was wise enough to know that the important thing was not whose side God appeared to be on, but rather on what happens when God is present in a fight. In the above story the leader knew that God would always let the weak and marginalized win, even if it meant that God would have to be defeated in the process.

The idea of the weak and oppressed having priority in the kingdom of God can be seen in the life of Jesus. Whenever Jesus favored the tax collector over the Pharisee or the Samaritan over the religious authorities he was not favoring one person or group above another because of what they believed. Rather he favored certain individuals and groups because of the social position they inhabited. In short, it was not

that Jesus had a deep love for tax collectors or
Samaritans over other careers and ethnic groups.
Rather, what was important was the place that
the tax collector and the Samaritan held in
society. Jesus was moved by the oppressed and
the excluded wherever he found them, always
seeking to reach out to those who had nothing
and who were considered to be nothing.

This story can be described as a pedagogical
tool designed to bring us insight into something
important about the life of faith. The fact that
God loses simply helps to solidify the importance
of the message. A similar example can be seen in
Matthew 15:22–28 when we read the following
exchange between a Canaanite woman and Jesus:

A Canaanite woman from that vicinity
came to him, crying out, "Lord, Son of David,
have mercy on me! My daughter is suffering
terribly from demon-possession."

Jesus did not answer a word. So his
disciples came to him and urged him, "Send
her away, for she keeps crying out after us."

He answered, "I was sent only to the lost
sheep of Israel."

The woman came and knelt before him. "Lord, help me!" she said.

He replied, "It is not right to take the children's bread and toss it to their dogs."

"Yes, Lord," she said, "but even the dogs eat the crumbs that fall from their masters' table."

Then Jesus answered, "Woman, you have great faith! Your request is granted." And her daughter was healed from that very hour.

Here Jesus appears to lose an argument. How are we to approach this passage? It would seem that Jesus wishes to teach his disciples an important lesson by taking their side and then allowing the woman to defeat him. In this way, the disciples are caught off guard. They think Jesus is on their side, but then they are faced with Jesus himself being beaten. Thus, the message is driven home in the strongest possible way: if Jesus is happy to admit being wrong, then so must we.

It is not difficult then to imagine the defeated army in the above story shouting at God because of their defeat, and God responding with a smile, "I'm sorry, I tried my best, but the powerless and the oppressed will always overpower me."

21

BETRAYAL

ONE DAY THE TEMPLE MASTER CALLED HIS YOUNGEST DISCIPLE TO SIT AND EAT WITH HIM IN PRIVATE. This disciple had been a devotee for many years and had carefully followed the ways of his teacher, learning to emulate the life of the Master as best he could.

But the great Master was now an elderly man and knew that he was close to death. He was fond of this disciple, yet he feared that the disciple was still some way from achieving enlightenment—not despite the Master's diligence but rather precisely because of it. And so, as they sat together the Master addressed his disciple, saying, "You have been a thoughtful and dedicated follower of my teachings for many years, and you may well one day become a great teacher. However, I sense that you are in danger of betraying me in your thoughts and actions."

"Never," replied the disciple in shock. "Since I was young I have followed your ways, never deviating from the path that you have ploughed. I never cease to reflect upon your words, and I never tire of engaging in the rituals and prayers that you have taught. I swear to you that I would never betray you, my great teacher."

"But you fail to understand, my young friend," replied the Master. "The fact that you have never betrayed my teachings, and the fact that you swear never to betray them: this is to betray them already."

■

COMMENTARY   ■

All great teachers will seek to nurture students who will surpass them. In order for this to happen, a painful separation must take place at some point between the student and the teacher. The authentic religious teacher is one who eventually asks his students to prove their devotion by finding their own way, moving beyond the lessons that they have learned, and taking responsibility for their own path. In short, the leader will one day say to the student, "Do not follow me."

Of course this is a strange, almost paradoxical teaching, for it is only by following the teacher that one will heed the command not to follow. Yet these words, when truly grasped, have the potential to set the disciple free, allowing her the chance to apply her learning in ever new and innovative ways.

This is not a betrayal in the sense of a rejection, nor is it a blind fidelity that seeks to live by the letter of the law. Rather, this loving move beyond the teacher in response to the teacher can be described as a faithful betrayal.

The teacher here is the one who says, "You will do greater things than I." This teacher stays only for a season so that the words, which act as bridge to truth, do not become a blockage to it, and so that their iconic presence does not morph into an idolatrous one. Thus, we can say that a total and complete fidelity to our teacher, an unthinking devotion to her words, will always end up being nothing but a betrayal.

22

THE BELIEVER

LEON HAD NEVER BEEN INTERESTED IN EXPLORING RELIGION. As a reasonable man, he considered faith to be irrational and damaging. However, one day a friend of Leon's was walking past a small church in the heart of the city and happened to look in. To his amazement, he saw Leon kneeling before some candles and mumbling a prayer. Leon had recently fallen upon hard times, so his friend guessed that this must be the reason for his newfound religiosity. But something seemed amiss, so he entered the church and approached Leon.

The sanctuary was dark and almost empty. Sure enough, there was Leon, crouched on the floor, reciting a religious incantation at the foot of the altar. Upon getting closer, his friend realized that Leon was reciting an old folk prayer that was believed by many to bring wealth and health to those who would recite it daily.

His friend was amazed and interrupted Leon, saying, "I thought you didn't believe in such superstitious nonsense. Do you really think that this prayer works?"

In reply, Leon looked up and angrily proclaimed, "Of course I don't believe it works, what kind of idiot do you take me for?"

"Then why are you reciting it?" said his friend, in shock.

"Ah," replied Leon, "it is because the priest informed me that this prayer works even if you don't believe in it."

COMMENTARY

In this story, Leon does not directly believe in the power of this prayer but rather believes in the priest's belief in its power. This may seem ridiculous, and indeed when put like this, it is. However, in many respects this is the kind of behavior we all engage in at some level. For instance, we can easily imagine a conversation between two people in which they agree wholeheartedly that working all the hours God sends in order to make money to buy more goods is detrimental to our mental health and not worth the effort. Yet it is also easy to imagine that, after the conversation, these two people act as if they did believe that working all the hours God sends to buy more goods is worth the effort. While the people do not consciously believe that this activity gives satisfaction and happiness, *they act as if they believe it*. Karl Marx called this activity of disbelieving in one's mind while believing in one's activities "fetishism." The fetish is any object that we know is not magical or special in any way, yet is treated as though it were special or magical.

In a sense, one can say that while individuals do not believe that working crazy hours for extra money in order to buy more goods will bring happiness, they have vicariously put their trust in another's belief that it does. So who is this "other" that believes on our behalf? It is, of course, not literally another person or group of people, but rather it can be described as the values expressed in the context we inhabit (the ads we watch, the books we read, etc.) While we may disavow these values intellectually, they continue to seep into our lives. While the message can be disbelieved and even ridiculed at a conscious level, it simultaneously commands our obedience at the level of our action. It is only as we change our context that we can effectively change our social existence.

Hence, the various religious practices employed over the millennia are not primarily designed to change how we think about the world, but rather, at their best, they are designed to change how we engage with the world. By developing a culture of spiritual rituals that reflect our beliefs, this new context begins to change how we operate in the world. Thus, it brings our beliefs and practices into closer alignment. We may believe very strongly in certain values, but it is only as we inhabit an environment that encourages those values, an environment that also "believes" in those values, that we are able to engage in lasting change.

Concretely speaking, then, when it comes to undermining something like the superstitious belief that a certain prayer can bring wealth and healing, the primary problem does not necessarily rest in convincing the person that this view is silly—that the words are only words and not some kind of magical formula that compels God to act. The chances are that the person will readily agree with this assessment. One needs to go further and convince that person's religious structure of the fact.

PART THREE

TRANSFIGURATIONS ■

23

BLINDNESS

NEAR JERICHO, a great scribe was sitting one day quietly reflecting by the roadside. As he contemplated life and faith, a large and noisy crowd stumbled by. The scribe became intrigued by all the activity, as this was usually a relatively relaxed and quiet place to sit, so he called out to one of the passers-by, "What's happening?" The man he addressed didn't stop, but shouted excitedly, "Jesus of Nazareth is approaching the city."

This wise man had heard much talk of Jesus, and so he eagerly joined the crowd. After some walking, everyone came to a halt, and silence descended upon the crowd. As the scribe looked up, he saw Jesus walking though the masses, talking with people and healing them. As he watched, a cry welled up from deep within him, and he began to shout, "Son of David, have mercy on me, a sinner!"

Those who led the way rebuked him and told him to be quiet, but the scribe shouted all the more, "Son of David, have mercy on me!"

As Jesus came near, he stopped and asked the man to approach. When the scribe came near, Jesus touched him and said, "Your faith has healed you." At that moment, the scribe was blinded and began to cry out like a fool.

When all the people saw what had taken place they were horrified, but Jesus paid no heed to them. Instead, he put his hand on the shoulder of the scribe and whispered, "You will be blind for a while." To this the man replied with a smile, "Oh, Lord, it does not matter in the least, for the moment you touched me I saw all that I ever needed to see."

■

◆   COMMENTARY   ■

The journey of faith is often described in terms of a passage from darkness into light, from blindness into sight. However, for mystic writers such as the late fifth-century theologian Pseudo-Dionysus, the more we attend to the source of our faith the more we realize how little we know. Indeed the word *mystic* itself is derived from the Greek verb *muo*, which refers to the closing of one's lips or eyes. It is also connected with the Greek word *mystikos*, which relates to the idea of having been initiated into the light. The result is a word that casts up the idea of closing one's eyes so as to be able to see.

This idea can also be seen at work in the life of the great philosopher Socrates, who is said to have been the wisest person in all of Greece, even though he claimed to be ignorant. His wisdom did not come from somehow dissipating his ignorance, but rather from knowing his ignorance and deepening it. While there is an unknowing that comes from laziness and lack of discipline, the unknowing of Socrates emanated from a lifetime of study, reflection, and dialogue.

We can also see this idea of a knowing unknowing at work in the life of Thomas Aquinas, the greatest of the medieval philosophers. It is said that, while celebrating Mass on December 6, 1273, he underwent an intense mystical experience. Upon leaving the church he proclaimed to Brother Reginald, "All my works seem like straw after what I have seen." He then set aside the work he had been undertaking on his *Summa Theologica*, believing it to be utterly incapable of describing the wonder that he had encountered.

In these examples, we witness the idea that faith is born from an event that is so luminous we are left dazzled by its incoming—an event so deep that we are saturated by it, so vast that we are dwarfed by it, and so bright that we are blinded by it.

24

THE FATHER'S APPROVAL

THERE WAS ONCE A YOUNG MAN CALLED CALEB WHO WAS OBSESSED WITH GATHERING UP POSSESSIONS AND GAINING STATUS. He was so driven by the desire to succeed that, from an early age, he managed to become one of the most prominent and influential figures in the city. Yet he was not happy with his lot. He worked long hours, rarely saw his children, and often became irritable at the slightest problem. But more than this, he knew that his lifestyle met with his father's disapproval.

His father had himself been a wealthy and influential man in his youth. But he had found such a life shallow and unsatisfactory. As a result, he had turned away from it in an endeavor to embrace a life of simplicity, fellowship, and meditation.

Caleb's father had taught him from an early age about the problems that come from seeking material and political influence, and he warned

Caleb in the strongest possible way to embrace a life that delves deeply into the beauty of creation, the warmth of friendship, and the inspiration derived from deep and sustained reflection.

Caleb's father was an inspiring man, well loved by all, and Caleb could see that his father, while living in a modest way, was at peace with himself and the world in a manner that his friends and colleagues were not. Because of this, Caleb often looked with longing at his father's lifestyle and frequently detested the path that he had personally chosen. Yet, despite this, he was still driven to pursue wealth and power.

It was true that his father was a happy and contented man, but he was also concerned about his son, and on any occasion when they spent time together, he would criticize Caleb for the life he had chosen.

But one day while Caleb's father was reflecting upon his son's life, a voice from heaven interrupted him, saying, "Caleb is also my son, and I love him just the way he is."

Caleb's father began to weep as he realized that all these years he had been hurting his son through his disapproval and criticism. So he immediately visited his son's house and offered a heartfelt apology, saying, "Please never feel that you have to change what you do or who you are. I love you without limit and condition just as you are."

After that day, the father began to take an interest in his son's life again, asking questions about what he was doing and how his work was progressing. But increasingly, Caleb found that he was no longer so interested in working the long hours. Soon he started to skip work in order to spend more time with his family and began to take less interest in what others thought about him.

Eventually, Caleb gave up his work entirely and followed in his father's footsteps, realizing that it was only after his father had accepted him unconditionally for who he was, that he was able to change and become who he always wanted to be.

COMMENTARY

Within the New Testament the apostle Paul writes, "The sting of death is sin, and the power of sin is the law" (1 Corinthians 15:56). In this poignant statement, he makes the claim that the law and sin do not sit at opposite sides of a spectrum, as people commonly think, but are intimately related. Here Paul understands that the law implicitly generates what it explicitly rejects. The more forcefully the law offers the prohibition "don't," the more its echo ruminates within our minds and heart as the temptation "do."

We can see this connection between the "law" and "sin" most clearly when we consider how prohibitions work in relation to children. For instance, when we say, "Don't open that cupboard when we are out of the room," we know that this command will likely generate a temptation to open the cupboard and will thus encourage the very action that it seeks to quash.

In this way, if we seek to overcome a certain behavior, it is no use embracing a law that condemns it, for such a law will only increase the temptation to engage in the behavior we are seeking to reject. The message of Christ informs us that it is love and acceptance rather than the law that sets people free.

One of the most radical elements of Jesus' life was not that he forgave and accepted sinners. This, in itself, was nothing new and would not have been in any way controversial or problematic to the religious authorities of the day. The religious authorities at the time would have embraced the importance of forgiveness and welcomed anyone who was truly repentant. The difference is that forgiveness is that which comes after repentance. In contrast, Jesus portrayed a radical forgiveness as unconditional and thus as that which is offered *before* repentance (see "The Unrepentant Son," below).

Jesus' understanding of forgiveness was so radical because he did not need people to repent before he would accept them. He did not require a change in their behavior before he loved, respected, and related to them. Yet, it was precisely this unconditional love and forgiveness that seemed so potent and transformative, often being the very act that drew people to repentance (a word that means to have a change of heart).

To the person who says, "I have tried so hard to change but can't," Jesus' response seemed to be, "It's OK, I love you and accept you just the way you are." Paradoxically, it is only when this message is taken to heart that real change can take place.

The law is abolished by love, and yet, in its being abolished it is also fulfilled. For once the law is swallowed up in love, then the temptation that the law generates loses its power and becomes impotent. Thus Paul does not say, *Your behavior is not permissible* but rather "Everything is permissible . . ." (1 Corinthians 6:12b). For, while the law enslaves, love sets people free to do what they desire, knowing that a person liberated by love will desire to live a life of love.

25

OVERTHROWING THE EMPEROR

THERE WAS ONCE A MIGHTY EMPEROR who had known only victory and prosperity during his entire life. Such was his success in battle and his absolute power over his subjects, that many considered him divine. The emperor ruled with an iron fist from a majestic palace built high up in the mountains—a vantage point from which he could survey his vast kingdom. Over time, he had built up the largest army that the world had ever known—an army before which every nation trembled. Yet, his thirst for power was unquenchable. He longed for an ever-stronger army and continued to oppress and torment his land with impossible demands for absolute obedience.

Yet, one night this great leader had a terrifying dream. In this dream he witnessed his vast army laid waste before him and his great palace in ruins. Then he heard a divine voice saying, "There is a heavenly power at work in your empire that can bring your whole army to its knees, a power that transcends your earthly reign."

The emperor awoke and said to himself, *I must see this divine power for myself.*

So he turned to the great religious leaders of his land, visiting their vast cathedrals and diligently engaging in all their elaborate rituals. He offered great sacrifices at the altar of the various gods and promised untold treasure to the religious authorities if they could reveal this divine power to him. However, no matter how hard he tried and no matter what rituals and incantations the religious authorities engaged in, the emperor felt no divine presence and witnessed no mighty acts. So he turned inward, seeking this divine power through private meditation, fasting, and prayer. He spent long hours practicing new forms of asceticism, prolonged periods of isolation, and every form of prayer he could discover. However, despite these great sacrifices, the emperor felt and saw nothing.

Then one morning he overheard two of his servants discussing religious matters. As he listened, he heard them speak of a great mystic who lived in the city. This man was believed to be so close to God that he could uproot trees and part seas with a mere gesture. As the emperor listened, he heard that this great man of God had contracted a terminal disease during his work in the poorer parts of the city. He was approaching death and had only days to live.

The emperor viewed this overheard conversation as a sign that God had finally heard his prayer, and so immediately, he called together an entourage of soldiers and servants, demanding that he be brought to the dying man's bedside without delay.

Within the hour, they left the palace, and, while the journey was long, they reached the city gates by nightfall. After some searching they found the humble dwelling of the old teacher, and the emperor boldly entered.

While the emperor rarely spoke directly to anyone other than his most trusted advisors, on this occasion he looked directly at the dying man and said, "I have been told that you walk close to God. I am here because I have heard of this God's power and wish to bear witness to it."

"Is that so?" replied the mystic. "I must warn you that the power of my God is unlike anything you have encountered before. If you truly seek it out, it will break you into pieces and destroy your reign over this land."

"So be it," said the Emperor, "if what you say is true, then fate has spoken."

The mystic nodded and then, with the last of his strength, beckoned the emperor to approach his bedside. The emperor complied, and in response the old man reached up, grabbed him by his fine robes, pulled him down to his knees, and whispered into his ear, "Here is the power of my God: it is to be found in my rotting flesh, in my weakness, in the dirt and disease of this world. You have not seen this power because it is in the people you have refused to heed; it resides in those you have tortured and put to death, those who have suffered under your hand. The power of God is to be found in the face of the widow and the orphan, in the illegal alien, and in the outstretched hand of the starving man. This weakness and fragility is the power of God, a power that can overturn the most evil of tyrants."

These were the last words of the teacher, for there and then he died in the arms of the emperor.

The emperor remained silent for some time, clutching the dead man's body. He looked around the humble dwelling and saw the poverty of the people who had stayed by this man's bedside throughout his suffering, and he began to weep.

COMMENTARY

By applying our understanding of worldly power to our understanding of the kingdom of God, we will form a picture of God as some great army general. Inspired by such an idea, the medieval church bequeathed to us what is called the great "Chain of Being," in which God is located at the top of a celestial hierarchy followed by angels, then kings and popes, through to bishops and priests, all the way down to the common people and to animals, before finishing up in hell.

However, the message of Jesus introduces us to a different way of approaching God—not as a violent power imposed from above, but rather as a powerless presence entering our world from below. This powerless God still instigates a revolution against the powers of this world.

However, this revolution is not won through brute strength, but through weakness. The Incarnation is a beautiful representation of this idea, for in the Incarnation we witness the rupturing of the human world by the divine world. Yet it is not a warrior who descends from heaven to disrupt earthly power, rather it is an infant who enters through the womb of a young woman. And it is this infant, rather than a warrior, who puts fear into the heart of the king and who shakes the very foundations of the world. In the Gospels we are confronted with an infant who grows into a man without a sword, a man who teaches his followers not to look for God in the palaces of the world, but in the dirt of the world—not in the well dressed and the well fed, but in the outstretched hand of a hungry stranger, in the naked flesh of a tortured body, in the figure of the thirsty, the homeless, the imprisoned (see Matthew 25:40). Here we are confronted with the idea that God is not encountered as the highest being in the chain of beings but rather in the lowest and most humble of things. This powerlessness and weakness constitute the otherworldly power of the kingdom, a powerlessness that can bring the most powerful rulers in the world to their knees. For, as Paul writes, "the foolishness of God is wiser than man's wisdom, and the weakness of God is stronger than man's strength" (1 Corinthians 1:25).

26

THE UNREPENTANT SON

THERE WAS ONCE AN ELDERLY MAN WHO HAD RAISED TWO SONS AND HAD WORKED DILIGENTLY HIS WHOLE LIFE. Now, the younger of the two sons was impetuous by nature and said to his father, "I do not want to wait for my inheritance. Give me my share now."

His father reluctantly complied. A few days later, the younger son packed his bags and departed from the home. For the next few years, he squandered the money that he had been given, leading a life of worldly pleasure. However, his money soon ran out, and the young son found himself without friends, food, or shelter. He eventually found a job feeding pigs and was so poor that he had to supplement his diet with the scraps used to feed the animals.

This was no life for the young man, so he thought to himself, *I have had a good time in the last few years, but perhaps I should now return to my father's home. For there it is warm, and while he will be angry, he may take pity on me and let me work as a hired hand.* And so he began the return journey.

But, while he was still a long way off, his father saw him. Overcome with joy, he ran to his lost son and embraced him. The father then said to his servants, "Bring the best robe that I own, and put it on him, and put a ring on his hand, and shoes on his feet. Bring the fattened calf and kill it, and let us eat and celebrate. For my son was dead, and is alive again; he was lost, but now has been found." That evening there was a great celebration.

Later that night, after the party, while he was alone, the younger son wept with sorrow and repented for the life he had led.

COMMENTARY

This is my second story inspired by the prodigal son in the Gospels. However, unlike the first ("The Prodigal Father," in Part One), this one sticks very close to the original. Indeed, I have merely changed a few features and excluded some others in order to unearth the radical message of forgiveness that is already embedded there.

Forgiveness is a word that has a lot of currency in our personal relationships, discussion in churches, political discourse, and even business affairs. Yet, the question we must ask concerns how much of what we baptize with the name *forgiveness* is really worthy of that name.

In politics when the word is used, we can assume something is afoot, and that there is a reason for the forgiveness being offered. One can assume that the word is uttered only after a variety of in-depth citizen surveys have been carried out and the legal experts have worked out a cost/benefit analysis. In short, this forgiveness is strategic and comes with conditions.

This is also true in the world of work. Here, forgiveness can be a great strategy for helping to ensure return business and a good reputation. Again, the word comes with implicit conditions. It is inscribed in a type of economics (whereby something is offered in return for something else).

Sadly, when it comes to religion, the same economic approach can also be seen at play. As

John Caputo notes in his book *What Would Jesus Deconstruct?* forgiveness all too often comes after a set of criteria have been met, namely an expression of sorrow, a turning away from the act, a promise not to return to the act, and a willingness to do penance.[3] Forgiveness thus *follows* repentance and so cannot take place until repentance has occurred.

This is the common understanding of forgiveness, and such an approach would have been welcomed by the religious authorities of Jesus' day. Religious groups have always loved repentant sinners. After all, there is nothing quite like parading a repentant sinner in church for inspiring the faithful.

But what if Jesus had an infinitely more radical message than this? What if Jesus taught an impossible forgiveness, a forgiveness without conditions, a forgiveness that would forgive *before* some condition was met? Now, that kind of forgiveness can really annoy people, and might help to explain why Jesus got a reputation for hanging out with drunkards and prostitutes (rather than with ex-drunkards and ex-prostitutes)! Indeed, it would seem clear from the

Bible that Jesus did not hang out with drunkards and prostitutes merely as a strategy to make them ex-drunkards and ex-prostitutes.

Yet is it not true that the unconditional gift of forgiveness, without need of repentance, houses within it the power to evoke repentance? As most of us know, it is often impossible to change until we meet someone who says to us, "You don't have to change. I love you just the way you are."

What if a forgiveness that has conditions, that is wrapped up in economy, is not really forgiveness at all, but rather is nothing more than a prudent bet? What if such forgiveness is like a love that loves only those who love us? What if repentance is not the necessary condition for forgiveness but rather the freely given response to it?

So, is this idea of forgiveness really what Jesus is talking about in the Gospels? Upon first looking at the original story of the prodigal son we might conclude that forgiveness is bound up in economy. After all, we read,

> When he came to his senses, he said, "How many of my father's hired men have food to spare, and here I am

starving to death! I will set out and go back to my father and say to him: Father, I have sinned against heaven and against you. I am no longer worthy to be called your son; make me like one of your hired men." So he got up and went to his father.

(Luke 15:17–20)

It would initially seem then that repentance in the story came before the forgiveness. Yet, is the younger son really repentant here? The text states that he came to his "senses," that is, he started to make a sensible calculation. One would have expected the narrative to claim something like, "in repentance he returned to his father's home," but the story describes the son's internal monologue as a strategic decision rather than a change of heart.

But even if this repentance were genuine, and not some kind of strategy that would allow the son to get a good meal and sleep in a warm bed, the father's response shows that no economy is at work in the kingdom. After all, we read these powerful words, "But while he was still a long way off, his father saw him and was filled with compassion for him; he ran to his son, threw his arms around him and kissed him" (Luke 15:20).

The father has no interest in whether or not his son is repentant. All he cares about is the son's return. In these lines, the Father is presented as having no idea what his son is thinking, and of having no concern about whether or not his son has a contrite heart. The father does not wait to see what his son says but simply embraces him in love.

The above story thus simply attempts to draw out the radical idea of forgiveness that is already embedded in the original story. It adds a conclusion that imagines how such unconditional love may have actually provided the power needed to precipitate a change of heart in the son, rather than his experiences of eating with pigs.

27

MANSIONS

AROUND A LARGE CAMPFIRE LATE ONE AUTUMN EVENING, JESUS COMFORTED HIS DISCIPLES by speaking to them of a heavenly realm that far surpasses the beauty of anything on earth. He spoke of a place that never grows dark or cold, a vast city that is filled with beautiful mansions, with streets of gold, and with unending expanses of green and fertile land—a place of perpetual peace and fulfillment.

Jesus spoke of this kingdom late into the night, painting pictures of heaven until the fire began to turn to ash and a chill filled the air. One by one, each of his disciples drifted off to sleep with the images of heavenly treasure and luxurious mansions feeding their dreams.

In the end only Jesus and a poor, unknown, and uneducated disciple were left, each one lost in thought, watching as the last cinders of the fire began to die.

After some time had passed, this solitary disciple looked over to Jesus and spoke.

"I was wondering about something," he said.

"Yes, my friend," Jesus replied.

"Well, there are so many people who follow you now that I can't help worrying that someone like me, an old, uneducated sinner, may get overlooked amidst all the great thinkers, politicians, preachers, and radicals who are being attracted to you and your message."

Then he turned his face away and continued, "I've never been in a mansion; in fact, I have never even seen one. So, I don't care too much if I miss out on all that. But tell me, will there be room enough for me when I die—will there be somewhere for me to stay in this kingdom of which you speak?"

Jesus looked at the man with compassion. "Don't worry," he whispered, in a tone that could barely be heard over the distant contented noises of the sleeping crowd. "Tucked away in a tiny corner of heaven, away from all the grand mansions and streets of gold, there is a cramped little stable. It doesn't look like much inside or out, but on a clear night you can see the stars shine bright amidst the cracks, and you can feel the warm breeze caress your skin. In this kingdom, that is where I live, and you would be welcome to live there with me."

COMMENTARY

It is easy for us to confuse the treasure of faith with the idea of treasure that we find celebrated by the world—a wealth that is concerned with material prosperity. When such ideas mix, we can be confronted with a religious message that promises wealth and riches both in this life and the next.

Yet the true wealth of faith does not lie with things that can rust and corrode; it does not manifest itself in the accumulation of even more products or bigger and better homes. The true treasure of faith begins and ends with love.

If we dream of faith leading to the accumulation of profit—as so many Christian preachers are quick to say on television, in great cathedrals, and in overflowing stadiums—we betray our deep-seated desire for a treasure that exists over and above faith. Yet, compared with faith itself, all else is but straw.

Indeed, the apostle Paul even went so far as to claim that the accumulation of spiritual riches is futile compared with the life of love, when he wrote, "If I speak in the tongues of men and of angels, but have not love, I am only a resounding gong or a clanging cymbal. If I have the gift of prophecy and can fathom all mysteries and all knowledge, and if I have a faith that can move mountains, but have not love, I am nothing. If I give all I possess to the poor and surrender my body to the flames, but have not love, I gain nothing" (1 Corinthians 13:1–3).

We can so easily miss the radical message that a life of simplicity is not contrary to the wealth of faith but is part of its very outworking. It is so easy to forget this and embrace the message of the world that the accumulation of success, worldly happiness, and possessions is a blessing to pursue. Thus, we give up the treasure we have for the poverty of affluence.

28

THE EMPTY EXCHANGE

SAMUEL AND LUKA HAD BEEN LIFELONG FRIENDS. Their relationship stretched back to when they were both children and continued through adolescence into their adult years. But their friendship really deepened when, during the war, they fought side by side in the trenches.

Yet, when they returned from the war, they both fell in love with the same woman. Although she finally married Luka, Samuel continued to harbor his own deep feelings for her.

As time went on, Samuel's parents were tragically killed, and he inherited his family's estate. Although now a wealthy man, he found it hard to accept the death of his parents and sought emotional support from the one woman he had always loved.

Amidst the intensity of the circumstances, a brief affair ensued between Samuel and Luka's wife. Unable to live with the secrecy of their actions, Samuel ended the affair and confessed all. Luka, devastated by the news, looked Samuel in the eyes and said, "Before God and all the heavenly hosts, I swear to you now that I will never accept your apology."

These words haunted Samuel for many years, for he felt awful about what he had done and yearned to be reconciled once more with his friend. Yet he understood the pain and heartache he had caused and knew that his friend was a man of his word. Samuel knew that his friend would remain true to his vow and would never accept Samuel's offer of repentance, even if Luka now wanted to.

Yet after years of wrestling, he decided that it did not matter whether his apology was accepted or not. What mattered was that he approach his friend and express his sorrow. So, early one evening Samuel gathered his courage and went to Luka's house. Upon seeing Luka, Samuel fell to the ground and cried out, "Old friend, I know that you cannot accept my apology because you made a solemn oath all those years ago. But I must tell you that there has not been a day when I have not been brought low by my actions. I have never been able to free myself from this pain, and I am truly sorry for what I did."

Luka smiled with compassion, for over the years he had come to understand that those had been dark days for everyone, and that Samuel had been suffering from great depression. So he addressed his repentant friend saying, "I made a vow never to accept your apology, and I intend to keep my word. But seeing you like this makes such an apology superfluous. Indeed, if I were to accept your apology, then this would mean that I considered you to have intentionally hurt me—something I know is not the case. So I reject your apology as unnecessary and thus keep my vow intact, not because I wish to continue our estrangement, but so that we can truly be reconciled as brothers once more."

After this Samuel and Luka were reunited and went on to grow old together as friends and companions once more.

COMMENTARY

Unlike "The Unrepentant Son," which looked at the issue of forgiveness, this story explores the theme of reconciliation. Here, in contrast to forgiveness, this reconciliation involves the offering of repentance as a prerequisite rather than a consequence. However, in contrast to what we might expect, the reconciliation here is effective, not because the heartfelt apology is accepted, but rather because it is rejected. Here we witness the idea of a gift that is effective only in its being refused by the receiver. Here Luka needed to hear the apology to know that Samuel was sorry. Yet the rejection of the apology shows that Luka understood the circumstances that surrounded Samuel's actions. In this act of offering a gift that is rejected, true friendship is thus restored.

Theologically speaking, one could say that, in a similar way, God utterly rejects our heartfelt apologies, knowing all the circumstances that caused us to do what we did. Yet it is only in the process of apologizing and having this apology rejected, that we experience the wonder of reconciliation. For we cannot have our apology rejected, and our relationship restored, until we offer that apology.

29

THE LAST SUPPER

IT IS EVENING, AND YOU ARE GATHERED TOGETHER WITH THE OTHER DISCIPLES IN A SMALL ROOM FOR PASSOVER. All the time you are watching Jesus, while he sits quietly in the shadows listening to the idle chatter, watching over those who sit around him, and, from time to time, telling stories about the kingdom of God.

As night descends, a meal of bread and wine is brought into the room. It is only at this moment that Jesus sits forward so that the shadows no longer cover his face. He quietly brings the conversation to an end by capturing each one with his intense gaze. Then he begins to speak:

"My friends, take this bread, for it is my very body, broken for you."

Every eye is fixed on the bread that is laid on the table. While these words seem obscure and unintelligible, everyone picks up on their gravity.

Then Jesus carefully pours wine into the cup of each disciple until it overflows onto the table.

"Take this wine and drink of it, for it is my very blood, shed for you."

With these words an ominous shadow seems to descend upon the room—a chilling darkness that makes everyone shudder uneasily. Jesus continues:

"As you do this, remember me."

Most of the gathered disciples begin to slowly eat the bread and drink the wine, lost in their thoughts. You, however, cannot bring yourself to lift your hand at all, for his words have cut into your soul like a knife.

Jesus does not fail to notice your hesitation and approaches, lifting up your head with his hand so that your eyes are level with his. Your eyes meet for only a moment, but before you are able to turn away, you are caught up in a terrifying revelation. At that instant you experience the loneliness, the pain, and sorrow that Jesus is carrying. You see nails being driven through skin and bone; you hear the crowds jeering and the cries of pain as iron cuts against flesh. At that moment you see the sweat that flows from Jesus like blood, and experience the suffocation, madness, and pain that will soon envelop him. More than all of this, however, you feel a trace of the separation he will soon feel in his own being.

In that little room, which occupies no significant space in the universe, you have caught a glimpse of a divine vision that should never have been disclosed. Yet it is indelibly etched into the eyes of Christ for anyone brave enough to look.

You turn to leave—to run from that place. You long for death to wrap around you. But Jesus grips you with his gaze and smiles compassionately. Then he holds you tight in his arms like no one has held you before. He understands that the weight you now carry is so great that it would have been better had you never been born. After a few moments, he releases his embrace and lifts the wine that sits before you, whispering,

"Take this wine, my dear friend, and drink it up, for it is my very blood, and it is shed for you."

All this makes you feel painfully uncomfortable, and so you shift in your chair and fumble in your pocket, all the time distracted by the silver that weighs heavy in your pouch.

COMMENTARY

This reflection was an outworking of my first interaction with the enigmatic figure of Judas. Here I wanted to play with our tendency to identify with the favorable characters in the Bible. For instance, when reading about the self-righteous Pharisee and the humble tax collector, we find it all too easy to condemn the first and praise the second without asking whether our own actions are closer to the one we have rejected than the one we praise.

Judas is here a symbol of all our failures, and Christ's actions demonstrate his unconditional acceptance. Judas helps to remind us of Christ's message that he came for the sick rather than the healthy, and that he loves and accepts us as we are.

30

THE BOOK OF LOVE

THERE IS AN ANCIENT LEGEND THAT SPEAKS OF GOD'S STRUGGLE TO GUIDE THE DESTINY OF HUMANITY. It is said that God had grown tired of the way that mortals constantly lose their way, creating disasters as they go. So he sent out his angelic messengers to gather together the timeless wisdom contained in the world and to place this wisdom into a multitude of books that would be housed in a great library—a library that mortals could use in order to work out how they should live and act in the world.

When, after many millennia, the great task was completed, the colossal library stood proudly in one of the world's great cultural capitals, dominating the skyline. However, this huge building contained too many books for any individual to read. It was all but impossible to reach for the majority of people, and the library's sheer size was enough to put anyone off even entering it. So God demanded that his couriers compress the essential wisdom into a single, encyclopedic book.

Once completed, this single work was widely circulated, but the manuscript was so huge that one could hardly lift it, let alone read it or put what it said into practice. So yet again God put his couriers to work, crafting a booklet with all the essential information. But the people were lazy and there were many who could not read, so the booklet was refined into a single word, and that word was sent out on the lips and life of a messenger.

And the word?

It was *love*.

COMMENTARY

This tale attempts to express the central message of Christ, namely love. All of the complex ideas, theories, laws, and creeds that are generated in the attempt to come to terms with one's faith can be boiled down to this one word and arise from it. It is this that we see being witnessed to when

Jesus is asked about the most important law. In response, he replies, "Love the Lord your God with all your heart and with all your soul and with all your mind" (Matthew 22:37).

Yet we must not forget that while faith is expressed in love, it is from a genuine desire to understand what this word concretely means at any given time that people develop various theories, laws, and creeds. The problem arises only when these provisional structures become unyielding.

It is love that should motivate us to create political solutions regarding environmental issues, social injustice, and ethical problems. But it is also love that should motivate us to question all existing political solutions, testing whether they really do deliver freedom and liberation. For the law is made for people; people are not made for the law. Without love political and ethical systems can become oppressive and unyielding. Without love we can become dogmatic legalists following holy books, sacred rites, and religious creeds without regard for their true purpose. This story simply seeks to remind us that the source of all our attempts to work out what must be done in the world should be love. It is love that calls us to build, and it is love that demands we tear down. It is love that calls the priest into existence, and it is love that calls the prophet to speak.

31

A MIRACLE WITHOUT MIRACLE

AFTER JESUS HAD DESCENDED FROM THE MOUNT OF OLIVES he came across a man who had been blind from birth. And his disciples asked him, "Rabbi, who sinned, this man or his parents, that he cannot see?"

Jesus answered, "It was not that this man sinned, or his parents, but that the works of God might be displayed in him. We must carry out the works of him who sent me while it is day, for night is approaching, when no one can work. As long as I am in the world, I am the light of the world."

Having said these things, he spat on the ground and made mud with the saliva. Then he anointed the man's eyes with the mud and said to him, "My friend, go, wash in the pool of Siloam." So the man went and washed and returned in jubilation, shouting, "I can see, I can see!"

The neighbors and those who knew him as a beggar began to grumble, saying, "Has this man lost his mind? for he was born blind." Some said, "It is the same man who was blind." Others said, "No, it is not, but he is like him." In response to this grumbling, the old man kept repeating, "I am the same man. Jesus anointed my eyes and said, 'Go to Siloam and wash.' So I went and washed, and now I can see everything."

To ascertain what had happened, they brought him to the Pharisees. "Give glory to God," they said. "We know that this man Jesus is a sinner." But the old man answered, "Whether or not he is a sinner I do not know. One thing I do know, that though I was blind, now I see."

But the Pharisees began to laugh. "Old man, meeting Jesus has caused you to lose your mind. You had to be carried into this room by friends, you still stumble and fall like a fool. You are as blind today as the day you were born."

"That may be true," replied the old man with a long, deep smile, "as I have told you before. All I know is that yesterday I was blind, but today, today I can see."

COMMENTARY

All too often the miracle of faith is reduced to the level of something that can be seen, touched, and experienced. The miracle of faith becomes synonymous with something like an unexplained healing, a prophetic intuition, or a resuscitation from the dead. Indeed, the word *miracle* is often used in newspapers when referring to such things as a lucky escape or an unexpected turn of events. In addition to this, some researchers have even attempted to test the existence of "miracles" through experiments that attempt to ascertain such things as the efficiency of prayer over the sick. All of these different approaches to the word view a miracle as a physical change in reality that cannot be explained due to the process of natural cause and effect.

One of the outworkings of such an idea concerns the difficulty, or impossibility, of ever being able to show beyond reasonable doubt that what has taken place is actually miraculous. As human understanding deepens, phenomena that we once would have thought of as miracles are now found to have natural causes. Thus it is always possible that what we think of as a miracle today could well be explained by empirical research and human reason tomorrow. The realm of miracles here is reduced to the ever-decreasing space of human ignorance. An understanding of our relative ignorance, combined with the existence of charlatans and our own tendency to cloud facts with our own hopes and desires, means that the idea of a miracle as a change in the physical world is always open to legitimate question.

However, there is another way of understanding the idea of miracle within Christian faith. This way does not rest upon such fragile foundations, nor does it banish the realm of the miraculous to the gaps in our understanding. This latter idea of miracle does not relate to a physical change in the world (though it may result in changes), but rather, it relates to a happening that cannot be reduced to sight, touch, or experience. Unlike the idea of miracle as that which is observed in the physical realm, the miracle of faith is not manifest in the external world. Rather it refers to a transformation in our inner, subjective world. In the miracle of faith everything changes in the life of the one who undergoes it. One is transformed, transfigured, reborn. While nothing in the world needs to change, nothing in the world remains the same.

This miracle is not something that can be denied by the one who undergoes it, for the miracle is testified to by nothing less than the fact of transformed existence. While the source of the miracle is open to question, the fact of the miracle is not.

This miracle is not an object in the world that can be interrogated by philosophers or dissected by scientists; rather, the miracle changes the way we see all objects in the world. This is the miracle of faith, and it is this miracle that all the stories of physical transformations mentioned in the Bible point toward. They are not themselves an expression of the miracle of faith; rather, they draw us toward it. If we take the spectacular transformations mentioned in the Bible as an expression of the miracle of faith, rather than as hints of the miracle, then we reduce the transformative event housed within faith to the mundane level of a spectacle. The true miracle of faith is too radical and precious to be contained there. For in it the whole life of the individual is liberated, healed, and saved, regardless of what takes place in the physical realm.

32

THE REWARD OF A GOOD LIFE

TWO BROTHERS EMBRACED FAITH TOGETHER AT AN EARLY AGE. One of the brothers took his commitment very seriously and wrestled diligently with the Scriptures. When he became a man he gave up all of his worldly possessions and went to live in the poorest and most dangerous area of the city. Many of his friends deserted him, and, because of his uncompromising dedication to the oppressed, he lost the one woman he truly loved, forsaking the possibility of marriage for the sake of his work.

The pain of this separation haunted him all his days. And because of the conditions in which he lived, he was frequently ill. When he died, no one was present, and only a handful of people showed up for his funeral.

In contrast, the other brother never took his faith seriously at all. As a man he became very settled, satisfied, and influential. He married the woman he loved, had many children, and lived in a beautiful home. As his satisfaction grew, his thoughts of God dissolved to nothing. He gave little to charity, unless it was prudent to do so for the sake of his reputation, and he paid little heed to those who suffered around him. After a long, happy, and successful life, he died in the arms of his loving wife with his children surrounding him.

In heaven God called the two brothers before him, embraced them both warmly, and to each gave an equal share of the kingdom.

As one might expect, the brother who had been faithful all his years was surprised—he had given up everything to live what turned out to be a torturous life of hardship.

However, his surprise was a joyous one. He turned to his brother, smiled deeply, and said, "Today my joy is finally complete, for we are together again. Come, let us break bread together." In response, his brother said nothing, but began to weep over the wasted life that he had led.

COMMENTARY

This is a story that interrogates our ideas of justice. In particular, it seeks to expose the deep-seated idea that to act morally is justified only by some kind of reward or recognition. The story's power is felt to the extent that the reader finds the equal reward given at the end of the story to be unjust.

We often think of God as one who delivers rewards in relation to how we act. However, what if the ethical act is in itself its own reward? Is this not how we should approach the selfless existence of the first brother, seeing him as engaged in a rewarding life that needed no external validation?

In addition to this, the story can help us to understand how change takes place in the kingdom of God. According to the wisdom of the world it would be wrong to give a great gift to someone who lived selfishly. However, is it possible that the very act of handing over a generous gift can encourage the receiver to become worthy of it? This idea is captured in the ancient wisdom that tells us how people are not lovable before they are loved, but rather become lovable when they are loved. For example, if, from an early age, we are shown love and affection, then we are more likely to grow into persons who evoke love and affection from others than if we are treated badly. It is as we are offered the gifts of grace, mercy, and love that we are drawn toward becoming persons who exhibit grace, mercy, and love.

In the above story the gift of God to the unworthy brother is precisely that which brings the brother to a place where he could finally become worthy of the gift. It is this gift that causes him to have a change of heart. The gift thus retroactively creates the conditions for its justification. That is, the conditions that would pave the way for the gift do not exist until the gift is given.

So then, whereas we might have expected the first brother to have been angered by the equal share of the kingdom and the second brother to have been overjoyed, the story turns this logic on its head. The first brother acted the way he did out of love (which needs no external reward) while the second brother, when confronted by unconditional love, is brought to his knees.

33

THE HERETIC

THE LAST PERSON EVER TO BE SENTENCED TO DEATH FOR HERESY was a young man accused of distorting the image of God by his false teachings.

As was the custom at the time, the accused was unceremoniously imprisoned and tortured in an attempt to extract a confession and repentance. But while the accused freely gave them a confession, he refused to offer repentance in relation to the charges. Perhaps, if they had continued, the torturers would have finally forced him to repent, but they did not care, for if the judge decreed a death sentence, then the apology would be extracted by the flames.

Once the prison guards had gained a written confession, the condemned man was brought before the court in order to hear his sentence. The judge listened as various people testified to words and images that the accused had used in explaining the ways of God. As was to be expected, the judge claimed that these teachings were misleading and could potentially lead to conflict and disagreement within the one true church. In light of this the judge decreed that this heretic must suffer death by fire in order that he might repent before passing to the other side and so escape the eternal flames of hell. Not only would this benevolent sentence bring salvation to the condemned, but also it would silence, once and for all, the false doctrines that he was teaching.

After the sentence was passed, the judge asked the heretic if he had any final words to say.

"One thing only, your honor," he replied. "I do not dispute your sentence. Indeed, I could not, as the charges made against me are quite true. And neither will I plead for my life. But, if it would please the court, on the day of my execution I would like to choose from among the gathered crowd the one who would light the fires upon which I am to die."

The judge thought for a moment, and then agreed to the man's last request. *It would be fitting*, thought the judge, *that one of the common people puts this man to death, for it was the common people whom this man led astray.*

A few days later, the time came for the execution to take place. As always, the stake and the bundles of sticks were prepared in the marketplace so that all the people could gather and watch the sentence being carried out. Since it was a bright morning, and the case was well known, a large crowd had gathered to watch the morning's entertainment.

Once everything had been made ready, the heretic was led through the crowd and tied to the stake, and the bundles of sticks were heaped around him. Once the people had settled, the sentence was read aloud to the condemned man. But before the executioner could set the sticks alight, the judge, true to his word, demanded silence. He then stood before the crowd and faced the condemned man.

"On the day of your sentence you asked if it would be possible for you to choose the one who would bring you salvation through the flames. I have not forgotten this, and so it is now time for you to choose who will have this honor. The one you point to will carry out this act by my word and by my authority."

As the young heretic's eyes darted through the gathered crowd, people began to feel uncomfortable. A dark and foreboding fear descended among the people, for the judge would surely demand that the chosen one light the sticks, something that no one wanted on their conscience. Slowly the entire crowd went quiet, until no one stirred.

When the whole marketplace had become silent, the condemned man gazed out into the crowd.

"I stand before you now, helpless as a child, condemned to death for heresy. I am guilty as charged, for I have held a distorted, muddied, and inaccurate view of the divine. I have only one request: that I be set alight by one among you who is innocent of this charge."

COMMENTARY

This tale was designed to resonate with a Gospel story that tells of Jesus intervening in a situation in which a woman, caught in adultery, was about to be murdered. Jesus responded to the situation by turning to those who were about to kill the woman and challenging them about the state of their own lives, saying, "If any one of you is without sin, let him be the first to throw a stone at her" (John 8:7). With these words the situation changed dramatically, for none of those gathered would wish to claim that they were without sin, a claim that would be patently false.

In a similar way, our heretic's words, whether heeded or not, turn the situation on its head. Instead of people being able to externalize their own failings onto another, thus rendering the condemned man into a scapegoat, the heretic demands that the people realize that what they are attempting to destroy is not external to them but rather lies embedded deep within them.

Here the issue concerns the idea of distorting the image of God. This young man has been found guilty of propagating a false view of the divine, and yet the young man knows this and freely admits it. However, he refuses to repent, for to do this would imply that there is a view of God that is not distorted, namely the view of the religious authorities at the time.

In this story we are led to ask whether knowing and admitting that one speaks inaccurately about God would actually be preferable to the claim that we can speak accurately about the source of faith. People may respond that this is all very well, but that some ways of describing God are healthy and some are unhealthy. Here I would wholeheartedly agree. The question here, however, is not how we judge between orthodoxy and heresy, but rather how we judge between good heresy and bad heresy. Another way of putting this is that we must question the difference between the heresy of orthodoxy, in which we dogmatically claim to have the truth, and orthodox heresy, in which we humbly admit that we are in the dark but still endeavor to live in the way of Christ as best we can.

■ ACKNOWLEDGMENTS

Mark Graham, for helping me find a suitable title for this book.

Mike Riddell, for being gracious enough to look over my first attempts at writing a parable all those years ago.

Anthony DeMello and Søren Kierkegaard, for renewing my love of parables and inspiring me to try my hand at writing them.

Paraclete Press, for supporting my work.

The Irish School of Ecumenics, for providing me with an office.

Ikon, the collective where many of these parables were born.

NOTES

1   *Before God and with God we live without God*   Dietrich Bonhoeffer, *Selected Writings*, ed. John de Grunchy (London: Collins, 1988), 291.

2   *The Writing of the Disaster*   Maurice Blanchot, *The Writing of the Disaster,* trans. Ann Smock (London: University of Nebraska Press, 1995), 141–142.

3   *What Would Jesus Deconstruct?*   John Caputo, *What Would Jesus Deconstruct?* (Ada, MI: Baker Academic, 2007), 73–74.

■ ABOUT PARACLETE PRESS

WHO WE ARE

Paraclete Press is a publisher of books, recordings, and DVDs on Christian spirituality. Our publishing represents a full expression of Christian belief and practice—from Catholic to Evangelical, from Protestant to Orthodox.

We are the publishing arm of the Community of Jesus, an ecumenical monastic community in the Benedictine tradition. As such, we are uniquely positioned in the marketplace without connection to a large corporation and with informal relationships to many branches and denominations of faith.

WHAT WE ARE DOING

BOOKS | Paraclete publishes books that show the richness and depth of what it means to be Christian. Although Benedictine spirituality is at the heart of all that we do, we publish books that reflect the Christian experience across many cultures, time periods, and houses of worship. We publish books that nourish the vibrant life of the church and its people—books about spiritual practice, formation, history, ideas, and customs.

We have several different series, including the best-selling Living Library, Paraclete Essentials, and Paraclete Giants series of classic texts in contemporary English; A Voice from the Monastery—men and women monastics writing about living a spiritual life today; award-winning literary faith fiction and poetry; and the Active Prayer Series that brings creativity and liveliness to any life of prayer.

RECORDINGS | From Gregorian chant to contemporary American choral works, our music recordings celebrate sacred choral music through the centuries. Paraclete distributes the recordings of the internationally acclaimed choir Gloriæ Dei Cantores, praised for their "rapt and fathomless spiritual intensity" by *American Record Guide,* and the Gloriæ Dei Cantores Schola, which specializes in the study and performance of Gregorian chant. Paraclete is also the exclusive North American distributor of the recordings of the Monastic Choir of St. Peter's Abbey in Solesmes, France, long considered to be a leading authority on Gregorian chant.

DVDs | Our DVDs offer spiritual help, healing, and biblical guidance for life issues: grief and loss, marriage, forgiveness, anger management, facing death, and spiritual formation.

Learn more about us at our Web site:
www.paracletepress.com
or call us toll-free at 1-800-451-5006.

◼ ALSO BY PETER ROLLINS

HOW (NOT) TO SPEAK OF GOD

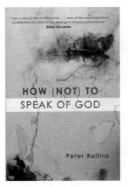

"Here in pregnant bud is the rose, the emerging
new configuration, of a Christianity that is neither
Roman nor Protestant, neither Eastern nor monastic;
but rather is the re-formation of all of them.
Here, in pregnant bud,
is third millennium Christendom."

—PHYLLIS TICKLE

"One of the two or three most rewarding books of
theology I have read in ten years."

—BRIAN MCLAREN *from the Foreword*

ISBN: 978-1-55725-505-1 | $19.95, 192 pages | Paperback

THE FIDELITY OF BETRAYAL

What if one of the core demands of a radical Christianity lay in a call for its betrayal? Employing the insights of mysticism and deconstructive theory, *The Fidelity of Betrayal* delves into the subversive and revolutionary nature of a Christianity that dwells within the church while simultaneously undermining it.

ISBN: 978-1-55725-560-0 | $19.95, 200 pages | Paperback

Available from most booksellers or through Paraclete Press:
www.paracletepress.com 1-800 451-5006.
Try your local bookstore first.